The

Magic

World

of

In-Laid

Pictorial

Tapestry

Constantine Issighos

Awaqkuna Books Inc.

NORTHWATER

Copyright 2008 © Contantine Issighos. Printed and bound in Peru. All rights reserved. No part of this book may be reproduced or transmitted in any form or by any means, electronic or mechanical, including photocopying, recording, and/or by an information storage and retrieval system except by a reviewer who may quote brief passages in a review to be printed in a magazine, newspaper, or on the web without written permission in writing from the publisher. For information, please contact: Awaqkuna Books Inc.

Northwater is an imprint of
Awaqkuna Books Inc.
www.awaqkunabooks.com

The Magic World of In-Laid Pictorial Tapestry

Library and Archives Canada

ISBN   978-0-9782018-4-5

Library and Archives Canada Cataloguing in Publication
This book was designed by the author.
Editing by L. Jacqueline Reid.
Interior Design, Juan Chávez, Josué Bautista
Peruvian University Unión, Peru

ATTENTION CORPORATIONS, UNIVERSITIES, COLLEGES, LIBRARIES, WEAVERS ASSOCIATIONS AND PROFESSIONAL ORGANIZATIONS: Quantity discounts are available on bulk purchases of this book for educational, gift purposes, or as premiums for increasing magazine subscriptions or renewals. Special books or book excerpts can also be created to fit special needs.

SPECIAL DEDICATION TO MY CHILDREN AND THEIR CHILDREN

Anna-Maria
Vittorio
Melissa
Jordan
Kaylee
Sabastian
Isabella

In memory of my son Robert who is no longer with us. We miss you very much.

ACKNOWLEDGEMENTS

Special thanks must be given to my friend Tono who introduced me to the art of in-laid Pictorial Tapestry. For this advice and patience, for showing me a better way of weaving and correcting mistakes, for the long walks and conversations we had over the future of the weaving art. My ever appreciation is offered in my most humble way.

I would never know the cause of Tono´s disappearance in that dangerous area. Where ever he is I hope he is in peace.

To Ulises Silva, Walter Rodrigues and to Julia Castro, whose long experience in in-laid weaving, in finding simple methods for accomplishing extraordinary results in both dyeing wool and weaving, has advanced me years ahead in my skills. Their presence will always be felt as I'm in-laying wool.

To the countless Native Fibre Artisants of the Sierras, who in one way or another have offered their advice and opinions over my style and choice of colours, I found their advice priceless.

Finally, to L. Jacqueline Reid whose attention to detail, sharp eye and skill helped complete this project.

A SENSE OF ACCOMPLISHMENT WHEN COMPLETING AN IN-LAID TAPESTRY FEELS LIKE. . .

- Catch a fish with your bare hands.
- Run the bulls in Spain.
- Witness a volcano erupting.
- Ride the world's biggest roller coaster.
- Visit the Taj Mahal.
- Make out on the beach.
- Laugh until your cheeks hurt.
- Visit the lost city of Machu Picchu in Peru.
- Skinny dip at noon.
- Do nothing.
- Run a marathon.
- Stand on the Great Wall of China.
- Bungee jump.
- Travel far, far away in a hot air balloon.
- Conquer your worst fear.
- Spend a week by yourself away from all forms of civilization.
- Learn another language.
- Learn to play a musical instrument.
- Fly a glider plane in the Grand Canyon.
- Remembering a moment's wish that was worth a lifetime experience.
- See the Aurora Borealis.
- Give a homeless person $100.
- Get a sexy tattoo on your _____.
- Take a chance and leave a job you hate.
- Spend the holidays volunteering in a soup kitchen.
- Reach 100 years of age.
- Plant a tree.
- Take a flying safari over Skeleton Coast, Namibia.
- Do all the above as a starting point.

TABLE OF CONTENTS

                                                  Page

INTRODUCTION 11

CHAPTER 1

Our Historic Artistic Legacy 13
The Artist of the Loom 24

CHAPTER 2

FUNDAMENTALS OF COLOUR AND COLOUR MIXING

**Fundamentals of Colour
and Colour Combination** 29
The Awaqkuna Colour Wheel 31
Mixture of Secondary Colours
Mixture of Third Order Colours (Tertiary) 32
**Mixture of Primary
and Secondary Colours** 34
Characteristics of Synethetic Dyes for Wool 35
**Preparation of Wool Before
 Synethic Dyeing** 35
Dyeing Process with Synethic Dyes 36
Preparing Synthetic Dye Powder 38
 Quantity (By Weight) 38
Calculation 39
**Dye Data for Synthetic Dye for Powder
of Stock Solution** 39
Formula for Colour Mixing. 39
 **Percentage of Dye Powder Needed
(Weight in Grams)** 39
**Formula for Colour Mixing: Dye Stock
Solution (Weight in Millimeters)** 41
pH 41

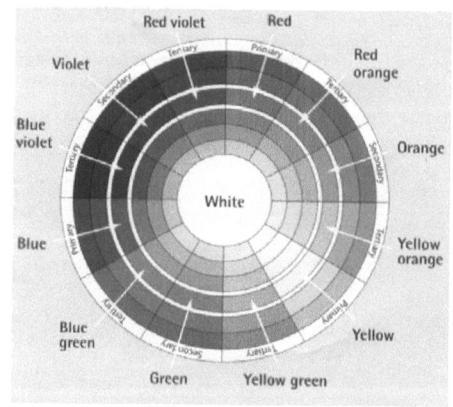

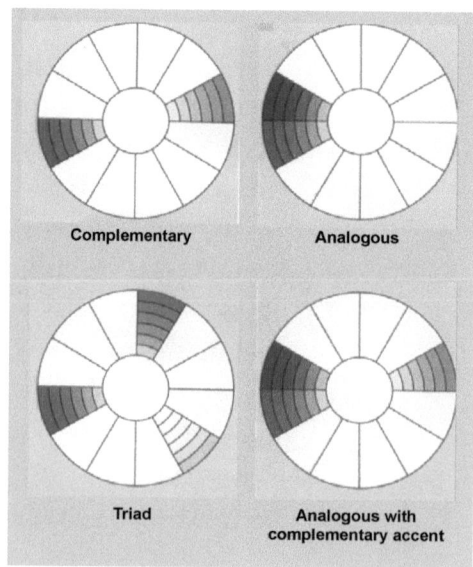

Auxiliaries for Vat Dyes: for Natural
   and Synthetic Dyes 42
Synthetic Dyebath for Wool 43

CHAPTER 3

DYER'S STUDIO

Fibre Characteristics of Wool 45
Sorting Wool 47
Teasing Sheep Wool 48
Washing (Scouring Wool) 49
Mordanting Wool 49
Drying Wool Fleece 50
Some Suggestions and Do's and Don't's 51
Storing Wool 51
Carding Wool 52
Hand Carding 53
Wool Carding Machine 55
A Dyer's Studio: Safety First 56
Good House-Keeping 57
Personal Safety Equipment 57
Dye Studio Equipment 58
Graduated Beakers 58
Graduated Pipettes 58
Weighing Equipment 58
Miscellaneous Equipment 59
The Art of Natural Dyeing 60
Some Suggestions About Dyeing 61
Collecting Raw Dyestuff 62
Preserving Raw Material 62
Dyeing Raw Wool: Brief Overview 64
Equipment for Natural Dyeing 66
Special Natural Dyeing Procedures 67
Preparation Procedures: Indigo 68
Process For Using Madder Root 69
Natural Dyeing For Success......................................70
Mordants 70
Measurements of Mordant 71
Custom Wool Dyeing 72

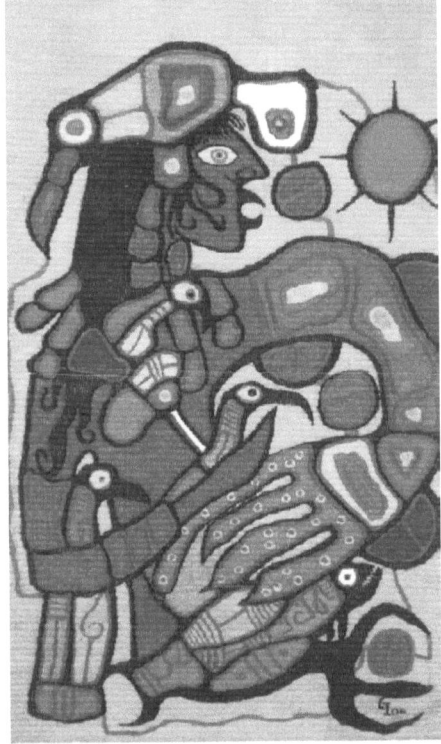

CHAPTER 4

FIBRE ARTIST STUDIO

Essentials of the Loom 87
Simple Framed Looms 88
Parts of the Frame 89
In the Frame Loom 90
Dressing the Frame Loom 90
Two Shed System 92
To Make Heddle Loops 92
Making Your Own Frame Loom 94
Winding the Shuttles 95
Warping 97
Winding the Warp 100
Walking Your Fingers and Chain 102
Removing the Chain Warp 104
Beater Reed 105
Roll the Warp 109
Tie-Up the Harnesses 111
Plain Weave, In-Laid Wool 111
 and Two Harness Loom 113
Profile Drafting: The Cartoon 113
Starting at the Beginning
The Use of Photographic Cameras
and Slide Projectors 113
Natural Perspective: Sketching Glass 115
The Use Of Photographic Cameras
and Slide Projectors... 117
Reproducing a Picture 118
Transfer Cartoon Onto Warp Yarn 119

CHAPTER 5

FROM LOOSE WOOL TO DYED ROLAG

Machine Carding Wool 121
Making a Rolag 123

CHAPTER 6

BASIC TOOLS AND THEIR FUNCTION

The Use of Metal Picker 125
General Observations 128
Temple Stick 130

CHAPTER 7

BASIC STEPS FOR TRANSFERRING CARTOON

Transferring Design Cartoon
Onto The Warp Threads 131

CHAPTER 8

PREPARING YOUR WARP THREADS

Preparing Your Warp Threads 135
Finger Carding 137
In-Laying Wool 138
Creating a Distinctive Sharp-line 140
Hand-Carding A Distinctive Line 142
Providing a Distinct Separation
Between Two Colours 143
Selvedge Protections 144
Removing Tapestry from Loom 145
Finishing Off Tapestry 146
Cross Warping: How to Avoid
Figure Distortion 147

CHAPTER 9

CREATING INTRICATE DETAILS

Creating Intricate Details 149
Special Effects 152

In-Laid Body Details 153
Adding Horizontal Lines 156

CHAPTER 10

THE BUSINESS OF YOUR FIBRE STUDIO

Marketing Your Pictorial Tapestry 157
The Ideal Business Location 158
Your Studio As Your Fibre Gallery 160
Turn Your Studio into a Classroom 162
Using Music 166
Media Exposure Of Your Studio 167
Using the Internet 171
Promoting Yourself and Studio
by Networking 176
General Observations of the Do and Don'ts:
What to Avoid 181
Is Consignment For You ? 183
Pricing Your Tapestries 185
How to Add Value to Your Tapestry 189
Symbolic Sgnature 189
Short Title 190
Date It 190

REFERENCE

ENGLISH & METRIC CONVERSION TABLES 192
ENGLISH MEASUREMENTS TO METRIC 193
CANADIAN AND AMERICAN HAND-WEAVERS'
ASSOCIATIONS 194
CANADIAN CO-OPERATIVE
WOOL GROWERS 201
GLOSSARY FOR FIBRE ARTIST STUDIO 202
GLOSSARY FOR DYER'S STUDIO 206
INDEX FOR FIBRE ARTIST STUDIO 209
INDEX FOR DYER'S STUDIO 210
A FIBRE ARTIST OF THE LOOM 211
FOR THE INSPIRED ARTIST OF THE LOOM 212
MY SIX-SIDED LOG HOME 213

INTRODUCTION

No word description however vivid and no photograph however true, can give a clear concept of the overwhelming obstacles that had to be overcome to make the Andean Sierras of South America accessible and habitable. The rugged terrain of the mountain system of the Sierras, the harsh climate and dense vegetation would appear to fit only for producing and sustaining a backward, poverty stricken people.

In such a geographical area, I first became aware of a simple folkloric artwork, in a form of woven tapestry. Depicting rural life, these tapestries were offered to passing travelers for a few coins. I too, bought one.

Later, as I was resting on a bed in a mud hut used as a hostel, I noticed that this 12"x12" tapestry on the foot of my bed was woven in a style not familiar to me. A simple curiosity lead me to further investigate the special technical characteristics, which made this style of 'weaving' so unique. I visited a local fibre artisan and observed how she was putting together her work.

I noticed that in place of weft thread in-laid wool was used to replace the repetitious work (back and forth) of the shuttle of spun yarn. Instead, natural dyed wool of assorted colours and shades were used to build up the tapestry itself. The shuttle was now used to interlock the cross woven space of approximately 3/8" wide, in-laid with dyed wool.

This special technique, in-laid wool instead of cross woven spun thread made this style extraordinary. What I observed was a method of woven in-laid with potential to inherent a dimension that could embrace multiple colours and background as intricate and artistic as a well composed oil painting.

Minute quantities of dyed wool composed of primary colours and background shades were given a shape and form in the palm of the fibre artist's hand. She then in-laid the shaped wool between the upper and lower level of the loom's warp (shed), and the shuttle was used to interlock the cross woven space. As the work progressed, these colour combinations slowly unveiled the artist's conceptualized theme.

What was needed on my part was to learn and apply this in-laid technique of (weaving) a Pictorial Tapestry to a more intricate style of western design.

Well, it was easier said than done. I've spent the next several years frequently travelling the high altitude of the Andean Sierras, learning, questioning, and arguing with other fibre artists. Style and application, colour, and shades, had to be modified. Old barriers of cultural misconception had to be torn down. It was a difficult time for me because I was confronted with cultural prejudices and mutual suspicion. The harsh nature of the Sierra region did not make my staying any easier. The high altitude of 4.860 meters above sea level made my normal breathing difficult. The heavy rainfall and the mudslides made the road to the region inaccessible to go in or out. All these factors, along with an intense political unrest contributed to more frustration.

In time, a much more homogenous artistic environment was created. Because of this crossing of cultures, a mutual respect and understanding was developed, and I was able to shed my own misguided phobias. Because of this achievement, I was able to master the in-laid method. Today after much time and trial, I am proud to present to you this book on the Magic World of In-Laid Pictorial Tapestry.

Chapter 1
OUR HISTORIC LEGACY

OUR HISTORIC ARTISTIC LEGACY

Like most narratives in the development of art, civilization and historical accounts, time's artistic link between our legacy and us starts along the banks of the Nile some 5000 years B.C. While weaving undoubtedly was practiced in many parts of the ancient world at a very early date, it was in Egypt, with its dry and hot climate, evidence of woven artifacts made of flax plant and of cotton has been preserved. Royal garments have been unearthed in tombs dated to the First Dynasty (c.3000 B.C.) and were used for mummy wrappings.

Later, the Egyptians were the first to develop and adopt the horizontal frame loom identical to the common floor loom in use today. Excellence in all facets of textile art continued until the decline of Egypt in the end of the second millennium B.C. Several centuries later the early Copts revived the art of pictorial weaving again.

While the Egyptian civilization and textile weaving was developing along the banks of the Nile, further to the east, another culture perhaps equally remarkable flourished in the land of Mesopotamia. Archeologists have unearthed clay tablets, some dated in the early 3rd millennium which served as account books for the weavers. In this area Sumerians, Babylonians, and Assyrians were all renowned for the quality of the textiles produced. Not only were the weavers highly skilled, they were specialized as well with each of the weavers responsible for a particular kind of textile.

Detailed accounts in the Old Testament describe of weaving practices by the Hebrews in the ancient land of Palestine. Wool and cotton linen fabrics dating from as early as 3000 B.C. testifies to the skilled fabric works performed by the weavers of the time. Strict religious Hebrew laws restricted the use of wool or the use of garments of mixed fibres as of woolen and linen together.

Hebrew weavers were divided into three classes: the common weavers of plain weaves, the weavers of multicolour garments, and the art-weavers who were regarded higher because of their decorative skills.

In the 16th century B.C. the textile arts were valued highly in the ancient Persia (Iran) as is evident in the architectural sculptures of the great cities of Persepolis and Susa. As commerce increased, Persian tapestries were widely exported to both Roman and Oriental worlds. By the 6th century of the Christian era, exquisite silk tapestries of rich colour and style had made their way in the European, Byzantine and China and to all parts of the ancient world. Persian influence lasted until the middle of the 7th century. This influence was declined when Persia was swept up with the rise of Islam.

Written and pictorial records of the ancient Greeks show that they were accomplished weavers of fabrics and tapestries, and other decorative arts such as embroidery. Their renowned mastery in the fields of architecture, sculpture, paintings, and pottery making tends to overshadow their weaving and textile artistic skills because of the absence of surviving artifacts.

However, the most famous recorded episode involving weaving in the ancient land of Ithaca, is the legend of Penelope, wife of Odysseus. Although Odysseus had been away on his voyage to Troy for many years, and presumed lost, Penelope continued to refuse the persistent efforts of many suitors for her hand in marriage. By day she would sit at her loom and weave, and by night she would unravel all the work she had done. This way she would not be forced to finish that shroud and urged to choose another husband.

Pictorial records show Penelope's work on a warp counter balance loom, and this was apparently the type of loom that was widely used in Greece, Egypt, Persia, and the Orient. Domestic production of wool was used for men's garments, while silk weavers from China and Greece would have also known Indian cotton from the writings of Herodotus.

When the Roman Empire absorbed most of the ancient cultures, the accumulative expertise of weaving skills aquired by various ethnic groups was at the disposal of the Roman conqueror. The high demand for fine garments by the aristocratic Roman families increased the number of fibre artisans involved in spinning, dyeing, and weaving by both house-slaves and free artisans. Those of lower social status who could not afford to own slaves for making garments for the members of their family, relied on free tradesmen who sold their fibre works in shops. Weavers' guilds were organized and proprietors -- displaying finished garments and wall hangings -- all done by spinners, weavers, and dyers were employed by the shop owners who occupied particular districts of town.

In the first century B.C. Chinese silk was introduced, and the first mixtures with linen or cotton formed the new kind of fabrics. Despite the painstaking effort to unravel the mysteries of Seri-culture (the cultivation of the silkworm and production of silk) Roman weavers were not successful. The secret was locked in China and in the early A.D., a pound of silk was sold for 12 ounces of gold. Much later when the supply of silk became plentiful the price of silk declined.

As Christianity became the dominant religion in the first three centuries, numerous converts were also made in Egypt. Among those who embraced the Christian faith were the Coptic's who, as members of an early Hebrew rebellious peasant class, were expelled from Palestine by the religious elite.

Coptic splendid textile art was particularly distinguished. Early Coptic fibre art achieved its highest development by the influence of flowing naturalism and highly

stylized forms of the abstract. Since Coptic's were primarily a closed peasant class, they rejected the cosmopolitan styles of the Romans and Hebrew elite in favour of more down-to-earth provincial mode. Figures of stylized animals, floral design and the tree of life were all characteristic motifs of the time. By the 5th century, Coptic Christian elements began to appear in the tapestries of the day with a story content and a richly emerged iconography had spread as far south to Abyssinia. Weavers, especially skilled in tapestry weaving created the first known tapestry mosaic –combining many small pieces of simple weaving in different colours.

Tapestry weaving known as **pile** that is, protruding strands of wool were also invented by the Coptic peasant class. The decline of the Coptic artistic tapestry was lost when the Arabs conquered Egypt in 627. Coptic weavers were recruited into the service of the **Moslim** caliphs. Interestingly, this resulted in the interwinding of Islamic motifs with Coptic forms. The prevalence of Coptic forms in Egyptian **woollens** endured until the 12th century, and so they retained the characteristics of their ethnicity.

From the above brief narrative, we can see that the history of mankind is written in the history of hand weaving and of creative utilization of the hand weaving artifacts is directly related to the early world's population, although much of the evidence is lost in the mists of time. Yet, artistic representation of early hand weaving is recorded at least 5000 years earlier in Mesopotamia.

Of humble origins, the earliest tapestry designs were often beautiful in pattern and colours. An art form, practiced originally by prehistoric artisans for clothing and by people whose necessity for a warm bed and against climate set an example for the future generation to come. Rugs to cover the bare floor of early dwellings and for comfort became cherished possessions.

In Egypt, China, India, and Persia hand woven artifacts and decorative rugs and tapestries slowly found a place and spread from house to house, from one farm to another, and from a village to village in the ancient lands. This is truly a remarkable history and one worth of more historical research and careful study. Looking also upon the ancient lands of the Nile and the Yangtze-kiang, we can find fibre artists of applied arts, 3000 years before the early Christian era.

It is thrilling to learn that early weavers wove fabrics for dress and decoration, and it is certainly interesting to also learn that they were masters of an art that spread quite rapidly, to early Europe and Arabian lands. The Coptic style of the 3rd century was woven in the same manner as the tapestries that were woven before the early Christian era.

Briefly viewing history of one ancient geographical area after another, it is easy to see that some textiles were exceedingly bold in their extravagance of material woven of wool, cotton, and silk and in many cases they were woven entirely of gold, silver, and even with jewels. Babylon the great, Egypt under the emperors, China and India; these ancient peoples all knew the arts of weaving, dyeing, and introducing symbolic figures, and geometric designs into weaving.

The art of pictorial tapestry has passed on through the ages and does no longer belong to a particular ethnic group. Mexico, Peru, and the Navaho Indians share the glory of weaving intricate pictorial tapestries which put them on par with the rest of the world's great weaving traditions.

In historical terms, each important event recorded in ancient times was depicted and expressed in the material product of its time, and it is in this that we can now study the development of fibre arts. Pictorial tapestries more than any other method of transmission has left us a pictorial history of events at a time when records were not kept frequently. The military expeditions of the crusades had a notable effect in the rise of the popularity of both European and Oriental designs. Travelling merchants of the time would return with tales of fantastic fabrics, gorgeous wall hangings and soft rugs of the Orient. These tales provide inspiration of the European rich with an interesting desire for luxurious goods.

By the 14th century, pictorial tapestries began to play an important part in the refinement of the day. Large wall hangings were now displayed in large cathedrals and monastic institutions. Clerical tapestries of ecclesiastical subjects such as the Apocalypse were displayed to promote their messages to their followers.

Homes of rich merchants of the time improved their households by covering their bare stone walls with marveled pictorial tapestries, which made their lives much less rude and, at the same time alleviated their social standing. Windows were covered with woven draperies, an open statement of wealth for all to see. Long before oil painting came to be, pictorial tapestries were the predominant decorative medium and transmitting method of social and cultural messages to the community at large.

My point is to demonstrate to you, as a novice weaver, that pictorial tapestry is not a craft. Hand-woven pictorial tapestry is an art with a recorded history that goes back into antiquity. It is an art that has stood the test of time and changes of artistic styles; with descriptive details and workmanship surpassing that of any oil painting of the 15th and 16th centuries. Oil painting became more popular because it was easier to learn, apply and quicker to complete.

Looking back into history we can witness the predominance of pictorial tapestry as a mode of representational still life. In the Metropolitan Museum of Art in New York, a 3rd century after Christ, a woman's head is woven in a typical Coptic style. Other rare woven tapestries of the same time period are housed in the Boston Museum of Fine Arts. Looking even further back at ancient decoration shows Penelope at her high loom, that is, four hundred years before Christ, and one still older shows an Egyptian weaving some three thousand years before Christ!

Pictorial tapestries departed from the original humble beginnings to become an esthetic luxury, a fantastic artwork, and a lively intoxication of wealth display by the upcoming political classes. By the 13th century the art of the loom was full of romance and fascinating figures of the past. By the 15th century, weaving of Pictorial Tapestry reached a high standard of artistic level, by its epitome with the skilful designs and weaving of the Great Masters of the Gobbling and Beauvais schools. It made it possible for later day weavers to identify their works of art by their tapestry marks left behind.

When viewing pictorial tapestries of the 13th century one can see that the high-warp loom was not changed from the early Egypt through Greece and Rome, and much later when adopted by the monastic institutions as far south as the Abyssinia monasteries. By the 15th century, weaving of Pictorial Tapestries reached a high standard of artistic level. At the same time, the high-warp loom was popularized in Europe by the widespread demand of decorative textiles. This popular demand shifted this artwork from the exclusive pictorial tapestries of the few to decorative need of the many. Colourful textiles were now covering not only windows, walls, and doors but people's bodies as well. Thus, hand weaving that was once nursed in churches and monasteries, public and private museums became a virile handcraft industry and bloomed into full production, beauty, and style from that time on until the 19th century.

The loom, on which pictorial tapestries were made, and which was known to humans as long as man's history, was now called the High-warp and the Low-warp. Yet, the weaving of the two styles of the loom was not differentiated by the weave alone. The low warp floor loom became popular in France and it was this type of loom that large studios hand wove tapestries on a permanent basis and under the protection of the royal crown. It remained for the low loom and the highest standards of weaving set by the weavers, which created a fine art associated with the perfection on pictorial tapestries. Studios of pictorial tapestries were not like workshops. They were more like schools, where the tasks at hand were done in concentration and silence broken only by an occasional voice of the Master Tapessier giving orders to his subordinates.

Between 1476 in France, Italy and Flanders, ecclesiastic Master-weavers were many and attained the dignity and ability of that position by creating masterpieces like **The Seven Deadly Sins** and other 'morality' subjects.

Religious superstition, pagan magic and mystical spells surrounded the making of pictorial tapestries. Popular beliefs concluded that in a house of pictorial tapestry a magic spell had fallen over it like the dew of morning to bless and protect all artists who had hand-woven in the loom. There was a strong conviction that in these studios there was some occult secret hidden within the looms that made it possible to create such masterpieces. Was this a way for the weavers of the day to protect their trade secrets?

Accessory to master tapessiers, and almost as important, were the natural dyers who prepared the dyes that were almost unaltered in colour after five hundred years exposure to light and air. Dyed stuff was precious during the Renaissance and the value of certain dyed wool and silks were not much less than the value of gold.

In the ancient world, weavers experimented with colour and dyes as soon as they were able to make their own textiles.

Fibre remnants dating from about 3000 B.C. were analyzed and found traces of indigo dye. The Phoenicians were advanced dyers and they were the first to experiment and develop the rare Tyrian purple dyes that for centuries only monarchs could afford. This exclusive purple was made from mollusk found by the coast of Tyre. Each gram of this purple dyestuff required fifteen thousand of the tiny bags, and this was the reason that only royalty could afford the high prices.

The term 'Palestine' derives from the Greek historian Herodotus who wrote that word as *Palaistine,* whose root lies in the Hebrew *Pelishtim* (Philistines) referring to the inhabitants of Phoenicia (Phoenicians) from the word Phonix, a Greek word for the dye purple. What's interesting is that the geographical area known, in the ancient times, as Poenicia, was also known as Canaan, an old Aramaic word meaning 'purple' because its inhabitants were famous for producing and trading in purple dyes.

A wide range of colours were available to the ancient dyers. Dye stuff like safflower yielded reds and yellows, and blue from indigo, red from madder. Red dye colour was used widely by the early Egyptians, the Persians, the Indians, the Greeks and Romans. Later, tiny insects found on the Kermes oak and the cochiniya found in South America cactus, both produced a popular red dye.

As far back as 2000 B.C. in the Far East, mordants were used, and it was this discovery of the mordants (the salts that combine with the dye stuff) that made the dye process leap into the future in the development of dyeing techniques.

In Europe the art of dyeing was highly secret, and the dyer's guild were there to protect these secrets. Such guilds prevailed all over Europe and regulated all arts and crafts. The great masters of pictorial tapestries and dyers belonged to their respective guilds, uniting themselves only by the work. It was the same protective guilds that in the end crippled or restricted the hand of dyers. The guild-laws were so complex and so numerous to comply with, in justice to their talent, and it was this talent with clipped wings that could no longer soar. Discrimination among dyers divided them into two main groups.

The Master-dyers whose dyeing involved the 'great dyes' which were to be madder-red, Crimson Violet, Green, Brown Tawny, Woad, and madder-black.

The 'second-class' dyers were those dyers who used the 'lesser colours' of brown, red, yellow and blue. One can only speculate the friction that must have existed among members of the same dyer guild and how they would share their trade secret recipes. The European upper classes were appreciating the high quality of pictorial tapestry. At the same time, however, the weaver and dyer's guilds were pressing their tapessier and dyers for more excellence. It was then that the guilds began to build a wall of restrictions and divisions on those who were practicing these special arts pressing to execute all the orders placed by the aristocracy. You see, by the 16th century the art of pictorial tapestry (with those brilliant colours) became of great demand. This was the time of the age of Romance, of Chivalry and of deep religious expressions. But this was also the age of the gradual decay of the art of the tapessier and the dyer from Brussels to Florence, Venice, Genoa to Guildhall in London.

Pictorial tapestries that were left for us (the new generation of tapessiers) to admire in museums are there to encourage us and dwell on the effects of the art of pictorial weaving had, and continue to have on the general development of the arts themselves.

Today with the ever increasing popularity of weaving in general, spread among the hundreds of large and small weavers associations all over the world, we must, once again revive the art of Pictorial Tapestry. We must not foster the feeling that only fibre artifacts should be produced or that this ever fast paced age is the front runner of our world's art progress.

We, the artists of in-laid Pictorial Tapestry must not economize time at the expense of expenditure of time demanded to create a perfect in-laid tapestry. Thus once again, we must enter and establish a brilliant period of creation like those tapessiers many centuries before us.

We must revive the passion in today's tapestry weavers to devote their lives to an art, which carries the long historical legacy of those unknown tapessiers in Egypt, Abyssinia, Mesopotamia, Peru and China, Persia and Navaho, and all those in far-off lands and of the centuries past.

We need once again to revive our historical artistic links, between our legacy and ourselves. We must establish a kingship with those weavers in Thailand and Laos, of Guatemala and Moroccans, of those in Middle, Far East and Europe, and we must make in-laid pictorial tapestry the common human link that know no national boundaries and ethnic prejudices.

I believe that gifted in-laid pictorial tapessiers would rise to the task, and inspired by their works, would produce such fibre art equal to their past legacy. The future fine in-laid tapestries must capture the public's heart, and cause a wonderful joy to their owners. The great pictorial tapestries of the past must become our natural inspiration, and a natural expression of our artistic passion. As all things large and small, the process is but the visible expression of an inward impulse, and we of the 21st century must revive the spirit that expresses itself in the inspired composition of in-laid Pictorial Tapestry.

THE ARTIST OF THE LOOM

An in-laid pictorial tapestry, according to the interpretation of the term used in the book, is a pictorial tapestry woven by a fibre artist in which the design is an integral part of it, depicting a subject that is not embroidered, stitched, or printed on its basic body. The in-laid tapestry's primary material is dyed wool with yarn as its structural interlocking of weft and warp.

With this flat statement, the term in-laid pictorial tapestry may be read without misinterpreting the term.

The term weaver means many things to many fibre craft persons; therefore, it is necessary to consider changing it to **tapessier** a term coined to fibre artists of wall tapestries in a time past when pictorial tapestries were at their highest perfection.

Following centuries of established fibre artworks, a contemporary in-laid tapessier is a passionate fibre artist, an artist whose design is of primary importance, one who chooses the right kind of dyed wool and colour, one whose sketch comes from her own inspiration. In short, an in-laid tapessier is a fibre artist with whom the loom takes the place of an easel, whose brush is dyed wool and whose colour medium is the dyestuff instead of oil paint.

This places the in-laid tapessier on a higher plane than that of a utility weaver, and makes the term seem appropriate.

Whether one is a utility weaver of practical used items or a tapessier, utmost recognition must be given to the natural-dye dyers whose conscientious craftsmanship keeps colour unaltered when exposed to light and air.

As a tapessier you must cultivate an open mind (avoiding having preconceived ideas) of what you want to create. You must always be perceptive to external impressions and stimuli, and the subjects will quickly present themselves and awake a response.

A chosen subject can be an attractive city or country landscape or part of it, which can equally strike a chord and challenge you. For example, a nocturnal street set, a humble piece of farm equipment by the barn, a rugged stone wall by the gate, an outdoor café scene, a country path or a lagoon may bring about something fresh and exciting. When you are able to separate a promising subject from a mass surrounding, this may have an irresistible appeal that can help you decide on the final composition. Pleasing composition, thus, must be held high on your list, and interplay of light, colour, tone, and shade must run a close second.

Take to task to create an intricate and understandable in-laid pictorial tapestry. Even if the task at hand appears beyond your learned abilities, taking it would not and could not be written by routine. Your desire to create an intricate pictorial tapestry, and simultaneously becoming an excellent tapessier, will be an expression of your own free will. Slowly and with focus and patience, you'll be accustomed to a kind of behaviour which, in time, will be good for your body and soul, and would be pleasant and fulfilling. Becoming a fine tapessier is a devotion, a relationship between you and your artistic creation.

Here, also we must ask whether there is a universal definition of what art is!! The obvious answer is, of course not! However, within the broad understanding of what art is, one can only interpret the art of in-laid pictorial tapestry on the basis of what is an understandable art and how it reflects life. A singer must choose her song theme that is understandable to her listeners. Otherwise, no one will have any clue what this noise is all about. A stand-up comedian is an artist whose aim is to make people laugh at her jokes. If both the singer and the stand-up comedian are incoherent to their respective public, then for whom do they perform? A self centered immature singer and comedian might claim that it is the public's fault for not understanding what these artists are trying to say. Well I don't know about that!!

Understanding something does not necessarily mean that one has to have a scientific knowledge about it. A customer walks into your studio and sees an in-laid pictorial tapestry with a theme that is understandable, but of course this person has no knowledge of the technical aspects of making that tapestry. Nor is it required for her to know. The same applies to you and I. In our daily tasks we use a cell phone, a computer, listen to a CD etc., all things understandable. Most of us are not familiar with the technology that goes with these things.

If a fibre artist chooses to make a tapestry with a theme that only makes sense to her, could this fibre artist claim that art is something of a universal mystery that is understandable to the gifted few? Is this what is called 'pure art'? Now if this 'pure artist' hangs such a tapestry in a gallery, does it need to be accompanied with a booklet explaining to the unfortunate what this art is all about? If this fibre artist wants to create 'pure' art, and never be concerned with whether or not this art will be sold, then this fibre artist can afford to be as pure as they want to be. You may conclude what you choose from this; but ask yourself, for whom am I creating this in-laid Pictorial Tapestry?

Someone once said, 'to create is divine, to reproduce is human'. Great skill and insight are required to create and reproduce a truly understandable in-laid Pictorial Tapestry theme. Transforming a simple idea into a skilful task of pictorial tapestry required a talent that takes time, focus, discipline, and effort to master. Using this newly acquired talent to create an understandable theme is a commendation to you and your chosen profession. Choose a theme that is understandable to all collectors, owners of diversified art galleries and the public at large. Study the Group of Seven, Van Gogh, Emily Carr, Kriekoff and others whose work of art theme can be inspirational to you. Themes these artists captured in their artwork were from everyday life and places. The art theme was a seascape, a neighbourhood, a landscape, a coffee house, Spring, Summer, Fall, Winter, a fishing village, a boat, a sunset, an old barn, a totem pole, a playground etc., all understandable.

Here, we must touch upon the subject of what constitutes a craft as opposed to an art. This we must do by including the notion of what an in-laid tapestry **is not!**

Traditionally works such as weaving, glassblowing, metalwork's, ceramics, etc. have been considered " minor arts", differentiated from the "major arts" such as painting and sculpture.

However the in-laid tapestries shown in this book, their intricacies and composition requirements were chosen to demonstrate that these tapestries are closer to the original paintings and sculpture, than works done in a conventional weaving of utility of conventional practical artifacts. These in-laid pictorial tapestries illustrated in this book, can definitely be classified as fibre artworks, for only a tapessier whose work requires the highest standard of colour composition, quality of material, ingenuity and workmanship, could create a true work of fibre art.: end of point.

The tapessier's profession, as one's life work, can now be re-established in a way quite different from the strict guild weaving of the past 500 years. In-laid design of pictorial works can undoubtedly change the subject matter of weaving more so today than ever. Esthetic designs of in-laid works that are based on the artistic manipulation of wool fibre, is open to a board venue limited only by the artist's imagination and workmanship.

For example, I've taken pictures of the original works by the Canadian Group of Seven, to drive the point to home! I've in-laid a number of pictorial tapestries out of these; though not 'identical' to the original paintings, nevertheless whatever limitations are evident can, and must be attributed to my workmanship rather than to the limitation of the medium. One thing is for sure; in-laid designs are at best in naturalistic imagery.

The illustrated in-laid pictorial tapestries in this book must not be thought of as copying or reproductions. Rather they are the creation of a new fibre artwork, derived from some other source, in this new medium!!

From whatever source of conceptualization (set in the tapessier's mind) in-laid pictorial tapestry is and will always be a personal expression on the part of the artist. You can glance at the illustrations in this book, and other fibre exhibitions and publications, and conceptualize how other designer artists have interpreted in-laid wool fibre as an art medium. There is absolutely no reason that you should not experiment with material, colour compositions, and style, that would deter, above all your individuality as an excellent tapessier of pictorial tapestries.

Chapter 2
FUNDAMENTALS OF COLOUS AND COLOUR MIXING

FUNDAMENTAL OF COLOUR AND COLOUR COMBINATION

Whether you are a beginner or an experienced dyer, you are always in need of more than one shade of the same colour. Some of these variations include the primary dye colours; Red, Yellow, and Blue. Secondary colours such as; Green, Orange, and Purple. With basic knowledge and plenty of experimentation, you can develop your own variety of colour mixture. Also, as long as you follow the directions and are careful when using measured amounts, you can make matched colours easier.

The advantage of experimenting with synthetic dyes is that is usually results in surprising variables of colour, tints, and shades. You may wish to learn to prepare dye stock solution for your colour mixes. Dye stock solution is dye in concentration.

THE AWAQKUNA COLOUR WHEEL AND HOW TO USE IT:

To make the dyer's life easier, colour experts have invented the Standard Colour Wheel. As you can see, in **Chapter page 5,** this colour wheel is divided into 12 equal parts, each representing a distinct colour. Furthermore, the colour wheel is sub-divided into 10 inner circles. The outer circles represent intensity of colour. The **intensity value** of colour is softened as you follow the scale towards the centre of the colour wheel, reducing colour intensity by 10% at each step of the colour scale.

The Primary Colours Red, Yellow and Blue are always at the same distance apart and are always in the same order. When you are mixing two primaries, you get a
Secondary: red and yellow make orange or blue and red will create violet.

Tertiary Colours (third order colours) are created when a primary colour is mixed with a secondary colour **next** to it on the colour wheel i.e., red and violet will make red – violet or yellow-green will make green-yellow.

Complementary Colours simply mean that they're **opposite** to each other on the colour wheel.

Triad means when all three primary colours, (red, yellow, and blue) are equi-distant from each other i.e., blue goes well with blue-violet and blue-green.

Analogous colours are located on either side of the colour wheel. When you add a colour from the direct opposite side, like an (secondary colour) orange, you'll get an analogous with a **complementary** accent. As such, you are creating your own colour scheme.

Present & Absent Black is present in all colours. White is absent of all colours. From the centre to the middle section of the colour circle, colour has low-intensity mixtures because they contain more white. The opposed is true as the present black is more evident towards outward of the colour wheel.

Tint refers to a colour with white added.

Shade refers to black added.

Tones refer to colour, such as, black, gray and white added to change the **Value** that is, the darkness or lightless of a colour. Following the scale of colour towards the centre of the colour wheel, the value of that colour changes accordingly. This is called **Monochromatic** i.e., many yellows placed together, each one softened by adding white. On the other hand, (analogous) neighbouring colours in the colour wheel will also create softer or less intense colours.

Finally, take your time to understand the fundamentals of colour and colour mixture. Test your understanding of colour intricacy with the following example:

You can choose complimentary colours from the opposite of two (2) neighbouring colours in the colour wheel; for example, yellow goes well with yellow-green and yellow-orange, that is the analogous colours that lie next to each other on the colour wheel. If you choose to add violet (a colour that falls opposite side on the colour wheel), what kind of **complimentary accent** do you now have?

The following guide will help you to choose the right colour accents when you are planning your next dye-bath. Once you comprehend how colours work together, this will give you the tool to create a more ambitious colour scheme for your next inlaid pictorial tapestry.

MIXTURE OF SECONDAY COLOURS

Blue and Yellow = Green
Blue and Red = Purple
Red and Yellow = Orange
Green and Orange = Brown

MIXTURE OF TINTS

Red and White = Pink
Orange and White = Flesh
Yellow and White = Pale Yellow
Green and White = Leaf Green
Blue and White = Pale Blue
Violet and White = Orchid

MIXTURE OF SHADES

Red and Black = Burgundy
Orange and Black = Salmon
Yellow and Black = Olive Drab
Green and Black = Deep Green
Blue and Black = Navy Blue
Violet and Black = Lavender

MIXTURE OF THIRD ORDER COLOURS (TERTIARY)

MIXUTRE OF…	COLOUR
Red, touch of Brown	Reddish Brown
Yellow, touch of Purple	Greenish Brown
Purple, touch of Brown	Deep Dark Reddish Brown
Brown, touch of Green	Dull Greenish Brown
Blue, touch of Brown	Deep Dark Brown
Red, touch of Brown	Dull Brown
Yellow, touch of Brown	Golden Brown
Orange, touch of Brown	Tobacco Brown
Green, touch of Brown	Myrtle Brown
Green, touch of Brown	Olive Green
Green, touch of Yellow	Light Green
Orange, touch of Green	Yellowish Green
Green, touch of Black	Dark Green
Green, touch of Purple	Dull Dark Green
Blue, White, touch of Violet	Arabic Greenish Blue
Green, touch of Blue	Greenish Blue
Orange, with black	Deep Orange
Yellow, touch of Orange	Yellow Orange
Orange, touch of Yellow	Light Orange

Purple, touch of Green	Light Dull Purple
Purple, touch of Blue	Bluish Purple
Red, touch of Purple	Reddish Purple
Purple, touch of Blue	Plum
Brown, touch of Purple	Chocolate
Blue with Orange	Dull Dark Gray
Green with Red	Deep Dark Gray

These are but a handful of dye colours. You can improve your dye knowledge and produce a set of recorded samples for future reference. As you go along, you may have projects requiring one or more of the above colours; this will give you a good start.

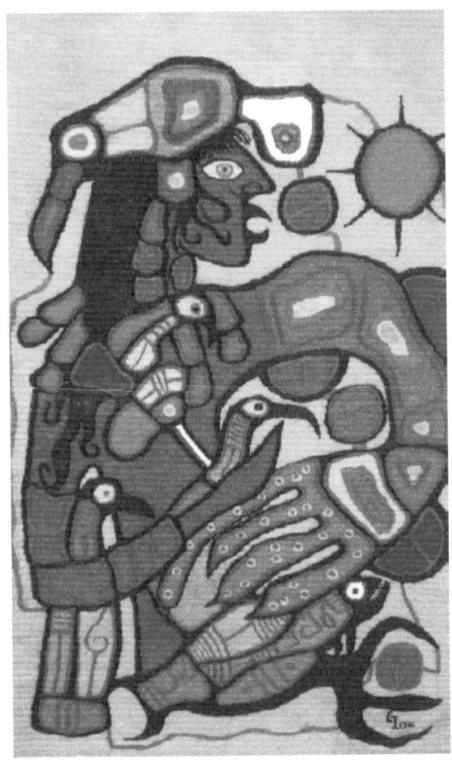

MIXTURE OF PRIMARY & SECONDARY COLOURS

The percentage of mixture varies depending on the depth of shade of one of the colours. The mixture may start from 50/50, 60/40, 70/30, 80/20, 90/10, 95/5 for deep colours. For more subtle colour-results you may try the formula 92.5%:7.5%, 97.5%:2.5%.

Try the following colour-mixture of Yellow-Purple, Purple-Yellow, Red-Green, Green-Red, and Navy Blue-Orange, Orange-Navy Blue.

Yellow-Purple	50/50	= Deep Brown	Purple-Yellow	30/70	= Soft Brown
Yellow-Purple	60/40	= Deep Brown	Purple-Yellow	40/60	= Light-Dark Brown
Yellow-Purple	70/30	= Medium Brown	Purple-Yellow	50/50	= Deep Brown
Yellow-Purple	80/20	= Medium Brown	Purple-Yellow	60/40	= Variation of Brown
Yellow-Purple	90/10	= Medium-light Borwn	Purple-Yellow	70/30	= Variation of Choc. Brown
Yellow-Purple	92.5/7.5	= Light Yellow Brown	Purple-Yellow	80/20	= Variation of Choc. Brown
Yellow-Purple	95.5/5	= Shaded Yellow	Purple-Yellow	90/10	= Purpleish Choc. Brown
Yellow-Purple	97.5/2.5	= Shaded Yellow	Purple-Yellow	95/5	= Purpleish Choc. Brown

Red-Green	30/70	= Earthly Brown	Green-Red	60/40	= Darkish Grey
Red-Green	40/60	= Choc. Brown	Green-Red	70/30	= Medium Grey
Red-Green	50/50	= Light Choc. Brown	Green-Red	80/20	= Greenish Brown
Red-Green	60/40	= Light Choc. Brown	Green-Red	90/10	= Forest Green
Red-Green	70/30	= Med. Redish Brown	Green-Red	95/5	= Swamp Green
Red-Green	80/20	= Redish Brown			
Red-Green	90/10	= Light Brown(magenta)			
Red-Green	95/5	= Medium Brown(scarlett)			

Navy Blue-Orange	60/40	= Dark Grey	Orange-Navy Blue	70/30	= Deep Redish Brown
Navy Blue-Orange	80/20	= Royal Blue	Orange-Navy Blue	80/20	= Medium Redish Brown
Navy Blue-Orange	85/15	= Deep Royal Blue	Orange-Navy Blue	90/10	= Light Redish Brown
Navy Blue-Orange	90/10	= Medium Royal Blue	Orange-Navy Blue	98/2	= Haiffa Orange
Navy Blue-Orange	95/5	= Light Royal Blue			

Note: Pre-mix Blue-Black 60/40 to create Navy Blue
Pre-mix Red-Golden Yellow 60/40 to create Orange

CHARACTERISTICS OF SYNTHETIC DYES FOR WOOL

Contemporary dyeing methods began in 1856 when **aniline** derived from coal tar, was discovered to be capable of producing a wide variety of colours when chemically treated. Subsequent research and further development released the dyer from his dependency on vegetable and animal dyes. Synthetic dyes of many different classes contain their own mordant. It may require the addition of a simple one such as table salt or vinegar, to be colourfast to light.

For our purpose, we will concentrate on those synthetic dyes whose chemical structure match that of the fibre of wool. i.e., Acid Dyes.

Acid dyes are of a type whose chemical composition is similar to sheep wool, silk, and other protein fibres. An acidic dye, in order to react with the wool fibre, contains ionic substances of moderate strength.

While household dyes or all-purpose dyes, may do the job, it is only those acidic dyes that will bond to the protein fibre in the dye bath. All others may give poor results for light fastness. Always check with the manufacturer's instruction and recommendations of dye auxiliaries. Lastly, most synthetic dyes are fast in their functioning and can be used without boiling. This last feature is important since boiling can cause wool fibre to felt.

PREPARATION OF WOOL BEFORE SYNTHETIC DYEING

Wool fleece needs weighting and scouring before dyeing. Place wool in a netting bag marked by its weight, number and other identifying markings for reference in a dye notebook. Identification of wool netting bags avoids confusion when preparing several batches of wool simultaneously. Do not overly tighten the netting bag; you want the dye to pass through all the fibre. Remember, wool felts with sudden changes in temperature, moisture and agitation.

DYEING PROCESS WITH SYNTHETIC DYES:

Synthetic dyes have come a long way, since they were introduced in the middle of the 18th century. Since then, research and development has led to the creation of many kinds and styles of synthetic dyes for all kinds of protein fibres.

Today, synthetic dyes that apply to our purpose of dyeing wool are as follows:
- All-purpose dyes, which are known as household dyes contain those dyes for both protein (animal) and cellulose fibres.
- Premetallize dyes to provide a strong bond between the dye and fibre.
- Acid dyes are commonly used to dye protein and other natural fibres.

A successful dye bath will, of course depend on you following the directions of a particular dye brand. Follow instructions and you become familiar with a dye's weakness and tintorial strength.

Step 1: Ask dye supplier or follow manufacturer's guide for quantities of dye and stabilizers.

Step 2: For dying wool make sure you are using **acid dyes** that react to wool fibre and may not need hue helpers.

Step 3: From your ready made stock solution take one cup of dissolve lye with a dissolvable sodium hydrosulfite.

Step 4: Dissolve all of the above into a small quantity of warm water.

Step 5: Prepare dye pot with 3-4 gallons of warm water. Add first the chemical stock solution following by the dissolved dye.

Step 6: Bring water temperature to 120F or 49C and immerse the net containing the wool fleece for 30 minutes or until desired colour strength.

Step 7: Lift the net bag with a hook and place net into a bucket of warm water next to the dye pot.

Step 8: Rinse with warm water **(thus avoiding felting)**, and repeat until wool is cool down. Remove wool from net and dry on a flat surface.

Remember that the lightness or darkness of a dye colour depends on the ratio between the amounts of dye used, the time of immerged wool in the dye pot, and the amount of wool weight.

PREPARING SYNTHETIC DYE POWDER QUANTITY (by weight)

In general, the quantity of synthetic dye required per dye bath will be stated on the dye's manufacture chart. However, here is table of calculations:

a) Measure the exact quantity of dye powder required.
b) Dissolve the dye in a plastic container by stirring in a couple teaspoons of warm water.
c) Water to dissolve the dye powder must come from the vat that is waiting.

CALCULATION:

WEIGHT OF WOOL(WOW) X LEVEL OF SHADE(LOL) = DYE POWDER NEEDED(DPN)

WOW		LOS		DPN
250gr	x	.2%	=	.5gr
250gr	x	.5%	=	1.25gr
250gr	x	1%	=	2.5gr
250gr	x	2%	=	5.0gr
250gr	x	4%	=	10gr
500gr	x	.4%	=	1gr
500gr	x	1%	=	2.5gr
500gr	x	2%	=	5.0gr
500gr	x	4%	=	10gr

The proration between the level of shade and weight of wool ranges from .2% (very pale shade) to 4% (deep shade). You may wish to create your own level of shade by following the above ratio suggestions of percentage.

DYE DATA FOR SYNTHETIC DYES FOR POWDER OF STOCK SOLUTION.

DYE%: refers to the percentage of dye needed in powder stock solution.
DYE POWDER NEEDED%: (DPN) a reference to weight of dye pwder needed per WOW, LOS, and VOW per dye stock.
% DSS: percentage of dye stock solution.
VOLUME OF WATER: (VOW) volume required per desired dye vat.
WEIGHT OF WOOL: (WOW) weight required per desired vat.
% LOS: refers to % of level shade ranging from .2% (pale), 1% (medium), 4% (dark).
VOW: Volume of water per 1% of dye powder.

Dye stock solution is based on the above 3 elements. LOS from pale to deep shade is directly related to the VOW per dye vat, and both determined the DPN for a succesful dye bath.

FORMULA FOR COLOUR MIXING. % OF DYE POWDER NEEDED (WEIGHT IN GRAMS)

WOW		LOS		DPN
100gr	X	1%	=	1gr
1000gr	X	1%	=	10gr

To create Navy Blue, for example, you will need,
1000gr X 60% = Blue (6gr) just move the decimal point.
1000gr X 40% = Black (4gr) again just shift the decimal point.

Ratio of VOW to WOW can be 10:1, 20:1, 30:1 or higher depending on desired results. Below is a simple formula:

you may wish to increase the colour concentration to a desired result.

VOW	MULTIPLY	LOS	EQUAL	DPN
100ml	x	1%	=	1gr
500ml	x	1%	=	5gr
1000ml	x	1%	=	10gr
2000ml	x	1%	=	20gr
100ml	x	2%	=	2gr
500ml	x	2%	=	10gr
1000ml	x	2%	=	20gr
2000ml	x	2%	=	40gr
100ml	x	3%	=	3gr
500ml	x	3%	=	15gr
1000ml	x	3%	=	30gr
2000ml	x	3%	=	60gr
100ml	x	4%	=	4gr
500ml	x	4%	=	20gr
1000ml	x	4%	=	40gr
2000ml	x	4%	=	80gr

Note: Do not add more that the required amount of one, element, unless you desire to change your ratio between all three elements.

FORMULA FOR COLOUR MIXING: DYE STOCK SOLUTION (WEIGHT IN MILLIMETERS)

For calculating colour mixing, the formula remains the same as above: volume of water x level of shade = Dye Stock Solution (DSS)

For example: a ratio between a primary colour of 60% to 40% (of a secondary colour) creates a tertiary one. (Percentage may change to the shade desired). To create your own Burgundy, you'll need 60% Red and 40% Black (if your level of shade is 1%) 1000ml of water.

1000ml x 1% = 10gr of total dye powder needed
1000ml x 60% red = 6gr of DSS
1000ml x 40% black = 4gr of DSS
(1000ml of mixed DSS to create Burgundy)

To avoid calculating errors, add both DSS amount together to confirm that the total agree. To reproduce the same colour (or any other), you need to know a) weight of wool b) the volume of different colour of DSS used.
The weight of wool is equal to the volume of the total DSS. Note: weight is calculated in grams. Volume is calculated in millimeters.

Remember for a minimal fee most manufacturers' can supply you with colour producing charts.

pH

The pH of the dye bath is important for a successful dye outcome. Acidic dyes require an acid solution to work with protein fibre. Most synthetic dyes will require an alkaline solution.

Alkalinity of a solution that is measured in a scale from 0 to 14 is called pH. The pH at mid point of 7 is called the neutral point, acidity increases as the scale decreases towards the 0 point; alkalinity increases upwards from the neutral point of 7 to 14.

Any reading on the pH scale that falls below 4 or increases above 10 must be avoided. This is in order to avoid fibre damage. Therefore, the scale must be corrected accordingly:

a) To increase the pH alkaline level of the dye bath, add an alkali (soda ash dissolved in water of alkali)
b) To increase the acidity level of your dye bath, add an acid i.e., vinegar

AUXILIARIES FOR VAT DYES: FOR NATURAL AND SYNTHETIC DYES:

Vat dyes require a special process to make the dye attach to the fibre. This is because vat dues, in both synthetic and natural state, are not water-soluble. There are two methods to convert these dyes to a soluble state:

a) Using chemical agent (sodium hydrosulphite), and
b) Natural fermentation (organic material).

Synthetic dyes can only be converted (soluble) by means of chemical reaction, therefore it requires:

1) Alkaline (lye) for the alkaline level.
2) Sodium hydrosuphite for reducing the oxygen present in the vat.

Follow your dye supplier's recommendation which alkaline agent is needed, and the appropriate amounts of both auxiliaries.

For natural fermentation, vegetable peelings (as agents) are put into the vat which, as the material decomposes and ferments, the oxygen. The alkaline level is achieved by using ash water or urine. If urine is used it is an organic substance, do not use ash water.

SYNTHETIC DYEBATH FOR WOOL

Step 1. Follow dye manufacturer's instructions about measuring quantity of dye and auxiliaries.

Step 2. Measure amount of water needed. Soak scouring wool overnight.

Step 3. Dissolve 1-½ teaspoons of lye into 1 cup of warm water. Avoid overflow caused by bubbling reaction in the solution.

Step 4. Add 1 teaspoon indigo powder into 1 cup of warm water. Stir and wait for the indigo powder to dissolve; add the reducing agent in the lye solution.

Step 5. Dissolve the required synthetic dye in a small amount of warm water. Set aside.

Step 6. Prepare dye pot(s) by adding dissolved dye with reducing agent solution and lye.

Step 7. At 120F/49C, immerse the wool while rotating solution for even dye distribution.

Step 8. Depending on the strength of the dye bath and the level of shade desired, keep wool submerged up to 30 minutes.

Step 9. Have available a plastic bucket close by the dye vat. Follow safety precautions i.e., wear rubber gloves, facial protection etc. Gently squeeze wool at the surface of the dye vat so that the excess dye remains in the dye vat. Transfer wool into the plastic bucket.

Step 10. Place dyed wool in a bucket of cold water, and rinse gently. Repeat rinsing as necessary. Let wool settle for 15-20 minutes.

Step 11. Submerse dyed wool in warm water with a mild detergent. Wash wool by squeezing gently.

Chapter 3
DYER'S STUDIO

FIBRE CHARACTERISTICS OF WOOL

Sheep raising was practiced throughout the ancient world. In Greece and Rome, flocks of sheep represented wealth and power, and from the earliest beginnings efforts were directed toward improving the quality and quantity of wool produced. Sheep's wool is the fibre most favoured by today's tapessier.

In the centuries since sheep were first domesticated two major changes in wool quality have been created by cross breeding; these are the loss of pigment in the wool, and the transformation from seasonal molting to the year round growth of fleece.

The Merino is one of the most ancient breeds of sheep. Most weavers and fibre artists prefer its wool, or have at least through the centuries. The Moors introduced the Merino into Spain from the African continent. Until the 16th century the Merino was not found in any other country in the continental Europe, but after that introduction to France, the Merino spread to other areas. In the 17th and 18th centuries, the Merino was introduced by Spain to her colonies in the new world.

The Rambouillet, also a superior breed for wool, was developed from the Merino. It has since become one of the primary breeds especially noted for its high wool yield. Among the numerous breeds of sheep grown around the world, there is considerable variation in fleece quality. Characteristics such as staple length, size of crimp, texture, strength, density, colour and dyeability are present.

Today dyed wool intended for inlaid tapestry come from breeds such as Cheviot, Columbia, Corriedale, Tunis, Vlahlia, and others. These breeds are noted for their excellent wool moisture absorption, which makes them dye-receptive to bring out the brilliance in dyes. Sheep wool presents a wide grade variation of fibre quality that can be found even in the same sheep.

As you can see in the drawing, the wool is finest on the head and shoulders of the animal and the coarsest on the hindquarters. The neck and dewlap produce the heaviest yield of fibres, while the whitest wool is around the head and neck areas (the finest) and yellow (the poorest) around the tail. The coarser a wool fibre is, the greatest will be its strength. Often the appearance of a particular wool fibre will be described in terms that compare its luster to silk or glass. For our purpose, the luster in wool brings out the brightness in dyes.

Wool demands special handling in the preparation stage. It is still possible to purchase untreated wool fleece from local co-operatives or individual sheep producers. Wool fleeces are available in several states. You can purchase whole fleece directly from a producer right after shearing, in which case the fleece will be **unscoured.** In most cases the extremely dirty wool on the outer edges of the stained fleece will have been removed, what remains is the **skirted_wool** whether the fleece has been washed commercially or artesian to remove part of the lanolin and dirt, the wool will be described as **scoured.** Large commercial producers offer wool that has been carded but not washed i.e., **greasy carded.** If washing includes carding, such as a wool is **scoured carded.**

Scoured wool that is ready to be carded is the only kind of wool that in-laid tapessiers use, where the lanolin has been removed, and the wool is ready to be dyed. Wool **roving** or **rolag** scoured wool can be purchased by the pound or kilo.

For the purpose of the inlaid tapestry making it is recommended to mix two grades of wool to produce a desirable text (softness) and strength, thus, one of the grades must be coarser than the other. Check with local wool co-operative and other supplier for the kind of wool they carry.

A local wool (sheep raiser) supplier is the best option to view the raw fleece first hand. If you purchase imported wool from a commercial washer make sure that they can certify that the end product is free of disease.

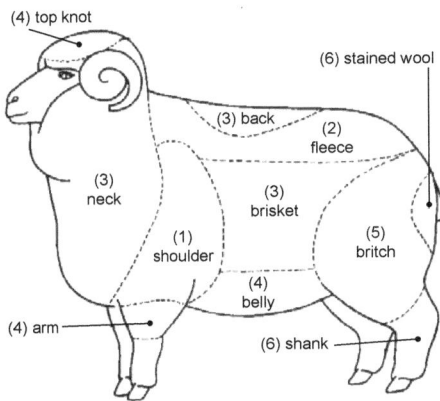

A note of caution: kemp describes the long, coarse and brittle hair (wool) found in some breeds of sheep. This wool does not accept dye. You should also avoid buying wool that is full of burrs or that shows fibre arranged in a disorderly manner. When you see such a disarrangement throughout the fleece, you can be sure that it came from a poor quality animal and should not be purchased.

SORTING WOOL:

Sheep wool or animal protein fibre purchased in raw fleece must be sorted for quality, separation of colour or stains from whites, length of hair, and removal of dirt and foreign particles before anything else is done. It is common in any raw fleece, to find sections in which some hair is longer than others and portions with finer and coarser fibres. Also, other parts of the fleece particularly towards the tail end of the sheep, which is or may be badly stained, makes it unfit to dye. Sorting therefore, is a necessary step to separate the longer fibre from the shortest ones, the whites from the colour ones, and the badly stained from the rest. Ideally, the sorting process should be done above ground, preferably on a horizontal screen or wire mesh, so that dirt particles and other matters can fall through and not recontaminate the wool.

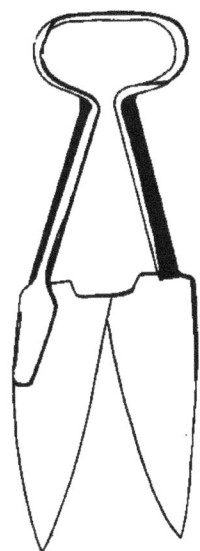

TEASING SHEEP WOOL:

Teasing is a process by which the fleece mass is initially opened up. Teasing also serves to remove dirt and other materials, and to blend the fibre thus distributing irregular fibre hair eventually throughout the mass of fleece. Sheep wool containing dirt, manure, and other material must be teased over a clean area. A proper and efficient way of working is to place the unteased fleece to your left hand side. With an area directly in front of you, you can tease (open up) each batch and transfer it to the right hand side. As you continue teasing, debris and dirt can fall to the ground.

Begin teasing by separating a handful of wool from the fleece. With a pulling motion from one hand to another, separate the wool gently avoiding breaking the fibre hair. The end result of teasing is to have fluffier and airy wool than the original mass. How much force you should apply in teasing wool would depend on the original state of the fibre. Densely packed areas in which dirt has become an integrated part of the fleece may need fairly firm pulling. Therefore, it is not uncommon that dirty wool could be teased more than once or until most of the debris is removed.

WASHING (SCOURING) WOOL:

Sheep wool must be washed after teasing, in order to remove the natural grease (lanolin) from it, as well as any dirt that remains on the wool after teasing. During the scouring process you must be careful to avoid felting because the conditions (for felting) heat, moisture, and pressure are all at hand. Avoiding felting is of primary concern, and it is for these reasons, that it is wise to subject the wool to a repeated washing in warm water while gently applying pressure. Do not try to speed up the washing process with too hot water and excessive pressure as the chance of felting increases greatly.

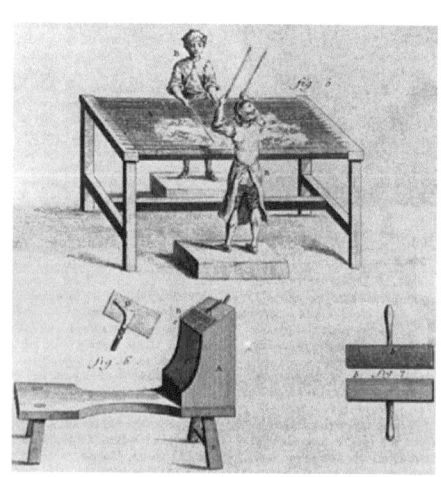

Scouring process for sheep wool is as follows:

- Fill the boiling pot with enough warm water to cover the wool and allow it to move freely. The ratio is two

gallons of warm water to 500 grams of dry wool
- Add to the solution, a water softener and a commercial wool scouring or a mild detergent. Stir until suds are formed. Note: if you are planning to have bright colours, a water softener is a must.
- Immerse the teased sheep wool in the pot and press down the wool as gently as you can circulating the scouring solution.
- Simmer at 120F (55C) for 30 minutes or until all dirt is removed from wool.
- During scouring check small portions of the wool to see that dirt and grease has been removed.

On a second pot:
- Add enough warm water at 120F to cover wool. Lift wool out of the first pot and place in the second. Rinse wool repeatedly and thoroughly.
- Cool the wool by rinsing until all solutions are removed, and at this stage you may want to consider mordanting.

MORDANTING WOOL:

Mordanting wool is a very important process to successful natural dyeing. Therefore, it must be done with care. Theoretically, a mordant is a chemical (salts) substance, which is added with the dyestuff to form a permanent colour. There are several methods for successful mordanting.

- To mordant before wool is dyed.
- To mordant while the wool is dyeing.
- To mordant before the after wool is dyed.

There are several advantages to each of the above methods. When the wool is mordanted before it is dyed, the colours are clearer, and there is more control over

the mordanting results. Some tapessiers who do their own dyeing, in order to eliminate one extra handling process, they prefer to mordant while the wool is dyeing. If you have two mordants to use, you can mordant before dyeing. This process will make brighter and stronger colours.

Should you decide to use this process, the second mordant should be only half the recommended dose. The basic colours will change if you use full amount of second mordant. Be careful to use the right dose of mordant.

DRYING WOOL FLEECE:

In order to dry the wet wool fleece, lay it out in the screen table, which would allow the water to pass through and dry, and at the same time, to allow air circulation through the wool. Make sure to set up the screen rack in a breezy area, and away from direct sun. Gently squeeze moisture out of wool, and turn it over once in awhile.

Once the wool is 100% dried, either place it in a plastic bag or continue with the dyeing process.

SOME SUGGESTIONS AND DO'S AND DON'TS:

- Wash wool inside a strong net bag if you are using a washing machine. Remove net bag when water is dirty. Fill the washer again and repeat process. Keep water warm.
- When you do the last rinse water add one-fourth cup of kerosene, it makes the wool fluffy. Odor of kerosene does not cling to wool.
- Make sure you use a very diluted detergent that does not leave an alkaline residue on the wool.
- Do not change water temperature suddenly.
- Do not subject wool to a high water temperature.
- Do not pour water directly on wool.
- Do not squeeze hard or agitate wool vigorously.
- Do not lift saturated wool above the water without support.
- Do not dry wool in direct heat or in an automatic dryer.
- Do not wash wool without water softener.

All of the above suggestions come from a long time wool handler from South America swearing of course by their own tried and true scouring and washing methods. You may wish to experiment a bit before deciding which of the above methods suits you best of all.

STORING WOOL:

You should not leave unwashed wool fleece resting in a container that you do not want stained with oil. This is because the oil in the wool, either natural or added, will seep into other material touching the fleece.

Greasy wool fleece should not be stored in an airtight container, because wool is a **combustible fibre.** Rather, you must store unwashed wool fleece in a dry place or in a porous container, such as a covered basket or a burlap sack. Do not store unwashed wool fleece in an attic or in an enclosed area, which may become overheated and cause spontaneous combustion.

If wool fleece is intended to be kept for a period of time, it must be scoured, dried, and properly stored. You must always be aware that natural grease in wool fleece becomes hard with time and the wool fibre turns weak. On the other hand, scoured wool will keep for a reasonable time without lost quality. Therefore, it is advisable to purchase wool fleece based on your next few projects. One suggestion, which you may find helpful, is to secure some large size glass jars with a screw top lids and store your dry wool in them. Do not put unwashed wool in jars. It is also advisable to place mothballs, repellents or other types of repellents to protect the dry wool in containers.

CARDING WOOL:

As with other animal fibres, sheep wool is also subject to at least one carding. Carding opens up the wool fleece mass to a greater degree of teasing. It also aligns, to some degree the fibres and helps with the final separation of any remaining debris particles while straightening the fibres.

Wool carders are wooden paddles onto which metal "spikes" are protruding to comb wool fibres. These spikes are bent at an angle for better combing. Carding is done by drawing the surface of one carding paddle across the other, by hand or machine in a movement that causes the wool to gradually transfer from one to another. Flat hand-held cards are always used in pairs. You may wish to own more than one pair, for carding to various degrees. The condition of particular fibres will dictate the carding's wire coarseness to be used. At times you must replace the carding cloth when the wires wear out.

HAND CARDING:

Place a layer of dyed fleece on the left hand carder (reverse the process if you are left handed). Then with well-stroked (smooth) movement of the left hand carder, begin the process of carding. Remember that only a small quantity of wool should be used at a time. If a section of your pictorial tapestry requires two different shades (of the same colour) now is the time to mix them. For example, if you have a green forest as a main background of your tapestry, you may use a deeper green with a lighter shade. Do not overly mix but leave one or the other shade in chunks within the overall colour. If you overly mix shades it would simply blend when carding. Place the bottom shade with another on top and stroke lightly. You will see streaks of the other shade within the darker/lighter colour. The actual carding process begins when the bottom card is

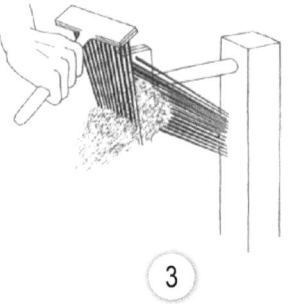

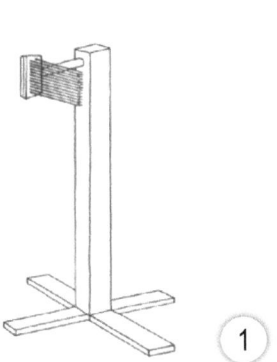

charged. Carding is a repeated process with two alternating steps—transferring fibres from one card to the other, and stripping. Stripping returns the cards to their condition of having one full card and the other empty, without disturbing the fibre flow. The amount

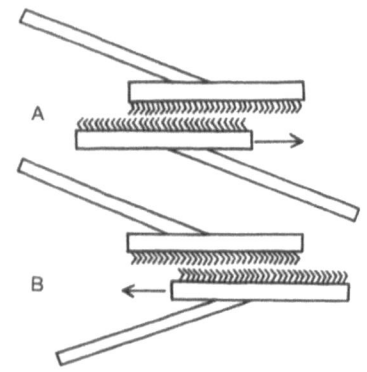

of carding necessary depends on how thoroughly the fibres were teased, the length of fibres, and the amount of fibre mixing to be done. Remember that the angles of wires on the carding paddles as they relate to each other, are important to the success of carding. In practice the cards must be held as close as possible for stripping, so that the wires would uplift the fibres. When

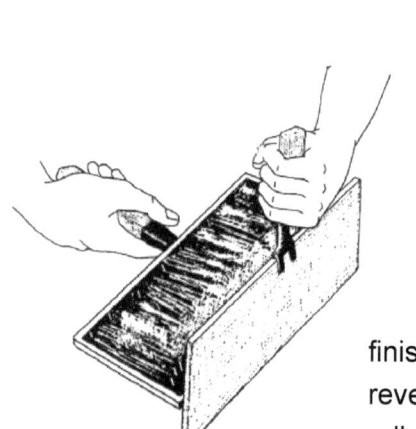 

finishing with carding, roll up carded wool-rolag by reversing the direction of carders and make a neat roll. Hang rolag on top of loom ready to be used or stored in a proper place.

WOOL CARDING MACHINE:

For the unhurried person carding can be a way of pastime. On the other hand, if you have a large amount of hand carding to do, you may consider seeking the help of a wool-carding machine. Once you use this, several pounds of wool may be carded in a short time.

Long hair wool fleece should be carded on the carding machine, because the wool fibres are better arranged parallel to each other, than the short ones.

The carding machine consists of two revolving drums, one small and one large, and a hand crank turns both simultaneously. The carding drums are covered with steel combs, similar to hand held cards. Teased wool is fed under the smaller drum, and after a few turns of the crank, the wool fibres are neatly carded batt on the large drum. When the large drum is filled with carded wool, a much smaller quantity of wool is collected on the small drum. Using a knitting needle you can now pry up the batt of wool along the width of both drums. Simply lift the carded wool off the drums and make a rolag.

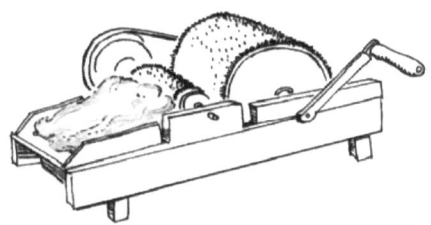

Others suggest cutting through the batt with scissors when it is removed from the drums, while others prefer prying off the batt, which leaves it with a better edge for joining, albeit uneven.

Remember to oil the carding machine as it operate, this will preserve it for a long time to come. Use light oil and keep the **carding pan** always clean from any remaining foreign materials that are carded out.

A DYER'S STUDIO: SAFETY FIRST

While natural and synthetic dyeing can be very rewarding and fun to do, it is also important that you must follow pertinent safety procedures to protect yourself, your family and the environment. It is of the utmost importance that you must follow these procedures and recommendations, in order to avoid injury. Special attention must be paid with hot liquid, all chemical fumes and splashes, and the handling of toxic dust on your studio floor. Under no circumstances sweep your studio floor, for you would inhale contaminated dust. Therefore extreme attention must be given to your overall ventilation capacity of your dye studio, making sure that it meets safety standards.

Seek information from various sources (on the Internet and from manufacturer's product safety) and do not assume that just because something is natural it does not contain harmful elements. Remember to keep your studio under a lock, especially if you have children around, and keep all chemicals out of children's reach, for the little people are very curious.

When you finish your day's dyeing project, remember to put away everything you have used and, as said previously, lock your studio's door for all the times that you are not using it. When mixing and measuring dye chemicals and powder ingredients, keep away from intake vents for both heating and cooling. Do not mix chemicals too close to direct heating and open flames. If you have a choice, do your dyeing outdoors rather than indoors.

GOOD HOUSEKEEPING:

- Wet mop your studio's floor when you finish with your day's task.
- Wipe clean all your countertops with a wet cloth or sponge, replacing those frequently.
- Do not wash your dyeing clothes with the house laundry. This would result in contaminating your normal laundry.
- Always use rubber gloves when handling dyes. If you have to use your bare hands, wash frequently.
- Wash all rubber gloves, aprons, and goggles and put away.

PERSONAL SAFETY EQUIPMENT:

- Disposable dust masks are very common protective gear and also economical. They filter out airborne particles and provide protection from evaporations and ordinary dust, but are much less effective than respirators.
- Air purifying respirators are designed to handle toxic fumes and can be found in both single and dual cartridges. Both can protect you from acid fumes, dust, and evaporations.
- If you are doing a lot of dyeing and you are in frequent contact with toxics, full-face cartridge respirators can protect your face and completely seal your eyes from toxic splashes.
- Wear protective industrial quality flexible gloves, aprons, face, and headgear. All these must be puncture resistant.
- For your studio's general safety, always keep a fire extinguisher near by an open fire or heat source. Choose a fire extinguisher that is above the grade of most home use types. Extinguishers for dye studio must be multipurpose.

DYE STUDIO EQUIPMENT:

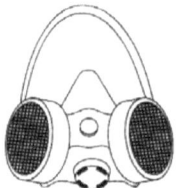

A variety of sizes of enamel pots and pans are needed for boiling and ronching dyed wool, and preparing dyestuff, as well as some canning pots for dyeing small quantities of wool. Several glass canning jars functioning as single dye pots for several colours are a quick way of heating simultaneously.

GRADUATED BEAKERS:

These are necessary for measuring solution and come in various sizes 50, 100, 250, and 1000ml. An assortment of sizes will provide you with the essential tools needed for both measurements and record keeping. Some beakers come in polypropylene (plastic); those are very economical and are heat resistant. Read labels to determine the degree of heat resistance, which should be about 200F/92C. I would not recommend Pyrex because they are very expensive (unless you buy them used) and break easily.

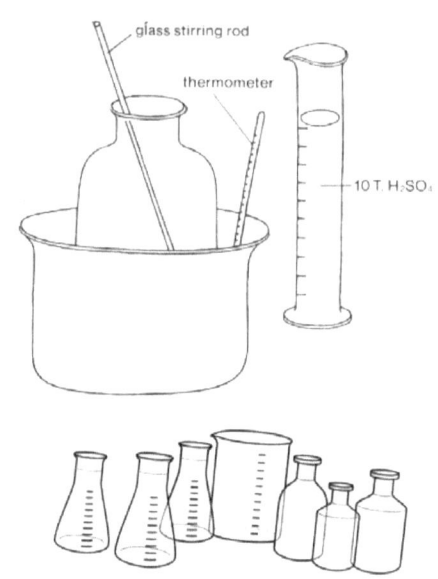

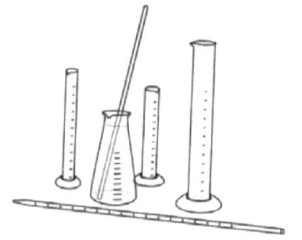

GRADUATED PIPETTES:

These are tubular glass units for measuring liquid in small quantities. For an exact pour of liquid use a syringe or a pipette built to fill-in. Do not use your mouth to fill them.

WEIGHING EQUIPMENT:

This is a must-have piece of equipment that has multipurpose: weigh dyes, wool, and natural dyestuff. A 500 gr weighting capacity should be enough for large-scale weight. For this you will need the counter balance type of scale. Digital scales or triple beam balance have a variety of weight capacity. Capacity varies with the model you choose.

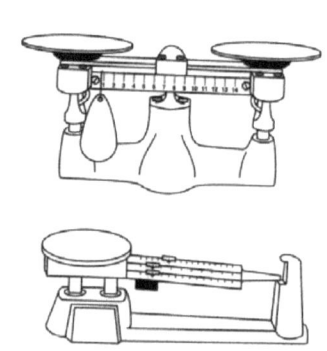

MISCELLANEOUS EQUIPMENT:

You'll need measuring spoons, glass syringes for transferring small quantities of liquid, wooden spoons (small and large), or dowels for stirring solution and for lifting wool out of the dye bath, chopsticks (plastic if you can) for stirring small quantities for dye solution, glass rods for your pipettes, a calculator, record keeping notebook, a small hand held coffee grinder to grind small quantities of dye stuff, a pH meter, thermometers, plastic buckets, scissors, mesh or netting bags to place-in for the dye-pot, paper towels, timers and a blender.

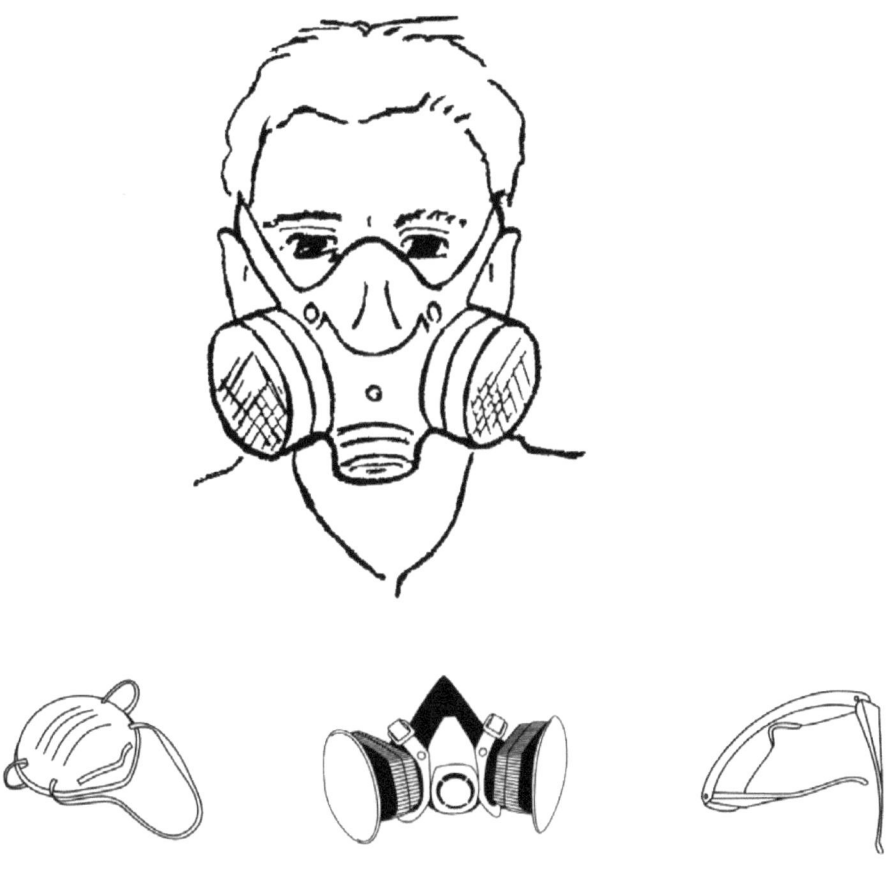

THE ART OF NATURAL DYEING

Since earlier times, dyer craftsmen have created a distinctive colour quality by using natural dyeing. An ever evolving craft, natural dyeing demands a level of knowledge, practical information, botanical experience, in the inspiration and performance relating to dye substances, fibre, and dyes.

Because of the variables involved, such as the various properties of the mordant and their effect on colour, or spread of the growing season, the seasonal conditions of a particular geographic area and the amount of rainfall, may produce unexpected results when dyeing. Other conditions may affect colour quality that may be quite different than the one expected. These would depend on the pH factor, heat, or whether the local water is hard or soft (rain water is naturally soft), the amount of sunlight and its effects on the plant, the method of dyeing, length of time in the dye pot, method of preparation; all these would often produce unpredictable results.

Mother nature, nevertheless has an abundance of colour sources for the dyer craftsman to choose; lichens and mushrooms, roots and bark, flowers and bugs, woodchips and stems are all available to provide them with beautiful bright or soft colours.

If you live in a big city and you do not walk the fields in the morning mist, you can find most of the dried natural dyestuff in craft stores, fibre suppliers, the Internet, and other sources. You can purchase alkanet, orange or Osage, Brazil wood, cochineal, cutch, indigo, logwood, and madder. Some of these come in powder or extract form. If you choose to collect your very own dyes try dandelions, marigold, white and red onions, all types of berries and black walnuts.

There is no comparison that, natural dyeing is quite more fun and much less expensive than commercial dyes. For many natural dyers, it is very gratifying and they take great pride in their craftsmanship. True enough, natural dyes are less predictable, colours and shades often fade over time. But for these dyers, it is still an intensely exciting and fulfilling process. The final decision to use natural or synthetic dyes would depend on you.

SOME SUGGESTIONS ABOUT DYEING:

There are several advantages in dyeing wool in large quantities. Choose your most frequently used dye colour for your next project. Calculate the amount of wool you will need and dye it in a single bunch. This will reduce the time spent per weight of wool being dyed. For our purpose of creating an interesting inlaid tapestry, dyed wool colour does not have to be precise. Uneven dyeing gives more presence to the colour of wool. Tapestry colour and shade background in landscapes appear much more lively, as well when you create different styles of tones and shades.

Shop around for the most economical mordant. Place it in the same vat with the dye. A combination of alum and cream of tartar is always preferable. With such a shortcut, your wool (with 10% cotton) can be washed, rinsed, and placed directly into the dye bath without separating, mordanting, and rewetting. This method would also reduce time and cost instead of double boiling the wool. Some experienced dyers prefer to use a combination of a mordant (alum only), with cream of tartar for every bunch of wool.

Both alum and cream of tartar are relative low in toxicity and most environmentally friendly. Some mordants and dye assistance such as sulfate and chrome, tin and oxalic acid are much more dangerous and a lethal dose can harm both adults and children. However, for your convenience, I have included several mordants including these toxic ones; it is up to you which ones you choose to use.

Finally, I have included a number of direct dyes (those dyes that do not need the aid of mordant and are water soluble): black tea and turmeric, black walnut and safflower (and others) that have a degree of fastness. You may want to take the opportunity to take this brief introduction in the art of dyeing, and expand it to the experience level you will feel comfortable. I recommend further reading on dyeing with both natural and synthetic dyes. You'll have a better control over the dyestuff and find it much more economical in the long run.

COLLECTING RAW DYESTUFF:

In general, natural raw material should be collected in peak season when plants, roots, and barks produce strong dye colours. Some natural dye raw material, those that can not be found in your area, can be also purchased from local commercial suppliers. Indigo, the bug-cochineal, logwood, madder, and cutch and some types of clays are commercially available.

PRESERVING RAW MATERIAL:

BLACK WALNUTS: Shell of the nut makes stronger dyes when they are still green with brown spots. Preserve as a shell or whole in a well-ventilated container until they are dry.

BLOSSOMS: Collect them when in full bloom, dry them in open air. Remember, that some blooms like dandelion and goldenrod must be used fresh.

ROOTS AND BARKS: It is best to collect them from trees or plants which have been removed: a good way to preserve the environment.

LEAVES, STALKS, STEMS, VINES, & TWIGS: All these should be air dried and stored in a well-ventilated container. You must collect them late in the season but before first frost.

BERRIES: You should pick them only when colour is dark and when they are ripe. Dry them one layer deep and turn them often. Store them in a well-ventilated container.

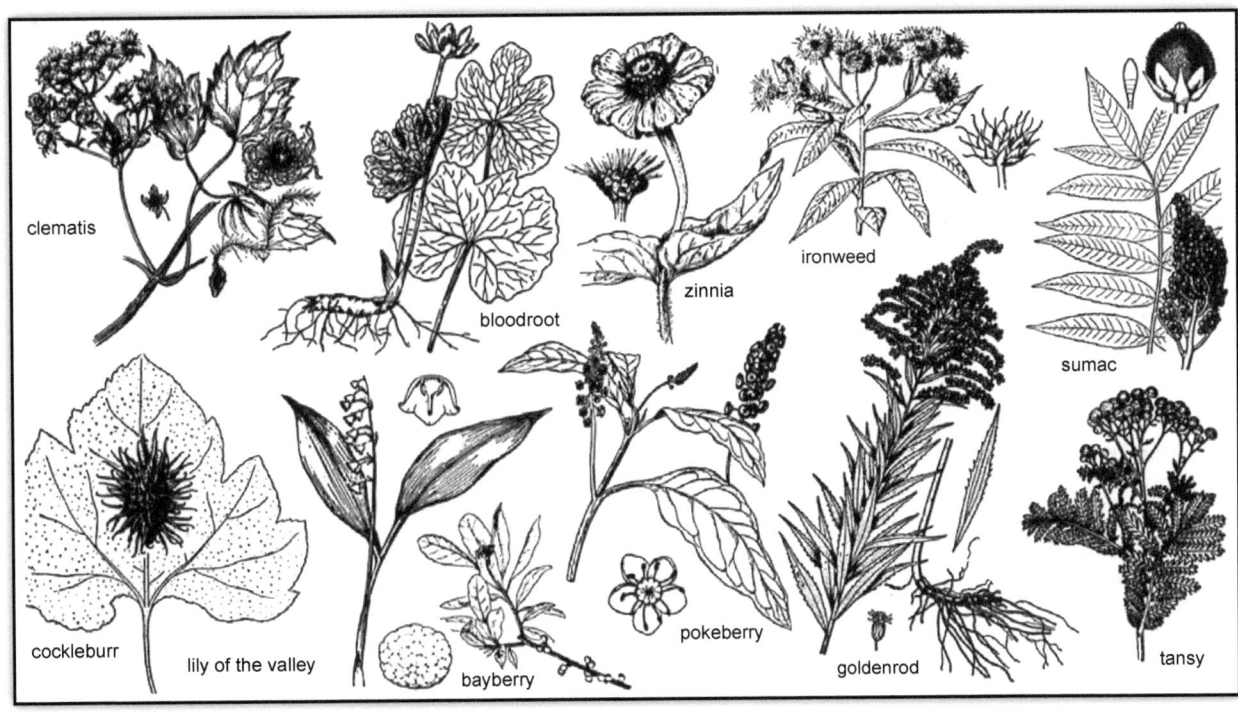

DYEING RAW WOOL: BRIEF OVERVIEW

Raw wool can be dyed by using the same recipes that apply to other natural fibres. Scoured wool should always be weighed when dried. Often, raw wool dyes to darker tones.

The natural oils in the raw fleece melt at low temperature and therefore should be kept below boiling point. It is advisable not to subject raw fleece to quick temperature changes. This will cause felting. Raw fleece that is very dirty and oily may have to be scoured more than once before it is clean.

Sheep wool presents the widest fibre characteristics depending upon the breed of sheep from which it was sheared. Different grades of wool can be also found in the same breed of sheep or even on the same animal. The deep folds of skin under the neck (dewlap) of the sheep produce

the heaviest yield of wool. Colour can also vary from one part of the animal to another. Wool is whitest around the head and neck areas, and stained around the tail. Always purchase wool that is all white in order to produce even dyeing results.

Weigh and scour wool before dyeing. For best results, place wool in a net bag for dipping into the dye pot. Do not over fill the net bag with wool; dye should be freely penetrating the inside of wool material. Prepare your dyeing process carefully. You'll need equal amount of dye pots, as many dyestuff is necessary. Make sure the synthetic dyes and stabilizers are non poisonous. Keep children away or under close supervision. Dyeing process is as follows:

- The amount of mordant required is 116gr of wool or 1 teaspoon of alum to 29gr of wool plus 1 teaspoon of cream of tartar.
- The amount of wool required for each bath of dye is equivalent to the dyestuff i.e., 50gr of dyestuff will equal 50gr of wool weight.
- Dissolve the amount of powder alum in saucepan containing warm water and the dyestuff; cover with additional warm water.
- In a net bag submerge the required wool and bring the contents of the saucepan to boiling point. For light colours simmer wool for 10-12 minutes (for darker colours 25-30 minutes).
- To give your wool deeper colour tone when dyeing you have a choice to either simmer wool longer or simply increase the amount of dyestuff in the dye pot.
- Repeat dyeing process for each individual colour or shade your project needs. When dyeing is completed for each colour, lift out fleece with a wooden spoon or a wooden stick and transfer into another pan and rinse with warm water.

- For much deeper colour you may wish to let wool cool down in dye bath.
- Allow fleece to dry flat on a towel.
- If you do not intend to use dried wool immediately, make sure it is well dried before storing it for later use.
- Well-dried wool should be stored in a well-ventilated container and put away.

EQUIPMENT FOR NATURAL DYEING:

Please pay attention to safety when using dyestuff, chemicals, and hot liquids. A well-ventilated area, preferably outdoors, is ideal to promote accident free dye projects. When using mordants, read manufacturer's instructions because some of these chemicals may be poisonous.

It is best to use an area specifically designed for your dyeing projects. Keep your equipment and supplies away from children's reach. Most of your basic equipment will be common kitchen items and will be easily found in your local flea market. Purchase these for the exclusive use of your dyeing needs and store them in a secure place; remember, however clean this equipment may look, never, never, never use it for cooking.

The following are some of the basic equipment that are needed for natural dyeing:

- A large pot (20 litres) with a lid.
- A large bucket for soaking and rinsing wool.
- A non reactive glass saucepan.
- Measuring spoons, large wooden spoons.
- A number of small jars or bottles for mixing mordants and dyes (stock solution).
- A pair of large tongs to handle hot wool.
- A pair of rubber gloves, masks, and goggles.

- A large working table and a drying rack.
- A small precision scale.

SPECIAL NATURAL DYEING PROCEDURES:

While most of the natural dyestuff do not require special handling in the dye bath, Indigo and Madder do require some interesting handling.

Indigo (Indigofera): One of the best natural sources of blue dye is Indigo which provides fastness. It is available from natural dye supplies in grains or powder form. Powder Indigo is not soluble in water; it must be dissolved (for dye extraction) by preparing a stock solution. The dye extraction procedure is as follows:

- 85gr (3oz) lye (caustic soda) dissolved in 1 cup of water. **Note:** Lye must always be added to water, and **never** the other way around, for it can cause an eruption.
- **CAUTION** concentrated sodium hydrosulphite is an extremely dangerous chemical, and serious burns can occur if you inhale its fumes or if the acid comes in contact with your skin. Protective equipment must be used, such as an air purifying respirator, eyewear against splashes, and rubber gloves.

Step 1: 225gr (8oz) plain table salt.
Step 2: 85gr (3oz) dissolved lye.
Step 3: 113gr (4oz) sodium hydrosulphite (sulphuric acid).
Step 4: 225gr (8oz) Indigo powder or grains.
Step 5: 950ml warm water.

This chemical stock solution, which is dissolved in a glass container, is sufficient for 4 1/2 gallons of dye bath. To help remove oxygen from the dye bath, and before adding the wool, sprinkle 28gr (1oz) of sodium hydrosulphite on the water.

PREPERATION PROCEDURES: INDIGO

The mixture of stock solution must be prepared outdoors or in a well-ventilated area. The utmost precaution must be taken when measuring and pouring chemicals.

- Only glass instruments must be used, such as containers, measuring beakers, and stirring rods. Do not use metal or wood for stirring chemical stock solution.
- Pour the acid into a glass container, and pour it against the stirring rod set in the middle of the container; this will help prevent spills as you pour acid slowly.
- Add the indigo powder and stir very gently. This may take a few minutes, as the indigo will resist dissolving. This will also cause the acid to become hot, so you need to make sure that the glass stock solution sits in a glass container with water at 100F, and must be held at a constant temperature while stirring the stock solution occasionally until the solution has turned blue. **This process could take up to two weeks.**
- Let the stock solution sit in a secure place. After two weeks the indigo extract is ready to be used.
- A word of caution: the indigo extract dye is very potent and it is absorbed quickly by wool and cotton fibre.

Ten days before planning to dye with indigo extract, allow 480ml of urine to ferment for the duration of allocated days, adding 113 gr (8 tablespoons) of indigo powder into the urine, and let mixture ferment for an additional 10 days totaling 20 days.

With one cup (225gr) of this solution extract you can dye 500gr of wool. Using urine is a traditional method for working with indigo. But if you find using urine offensive, use vegetable peelings or Madder root added to the bath, thus allowing decomposition and fermentation. In this case you can eliminate urine.

PROCESS FOR USING MADDER ROOT:

One of the strange characteristics of madder is that it prefers hard to soft water. This root is much less complicated to work with than indigo. Madder roots contain both red and brown dye substance. Which one of these hues you will want to be released depends on the water's temperature. (See below). To prepare a dye bath with Madder roots follow the steps in this order:

Step 1: Cut ½ pound (500gr) of Madder roots into small pieces.

Step 2: Cover roots with two (2) gallons of water.

Step 3: Bring water temperature up very slowly over a period of one hour, until it is just below simmering point.

Step 4: At below simmering point, a red dye will be released. At boiling point a brown dye will be released.

Step5: Maintain water temperature under simmering point until red dye is extracted. Remove all waste material.

Step 6: Add a third gallon of warm water into the dye pot and immerse the wool.

Step 7: Maintain the dye bath under simmering point for 20 minutes or until desired colour is achieved. Remember, if the dye bath is boiling, the solution will turn brown.

Step8: Follow mordanting procedure of dyeing wool fleece.

NATURAL DYEING FOR SUCCESS

Many large fibre stores and other suppliers carry a variety of natural and synthetic dyes that are in dry or in liquid forms. Both kinds of dyes produce fairly consistent results, as long as you follow the directions and you are careful when using measured amounts. Dyes are available in a variety of colours which makes mixed and matched colours easier. Some of these are:

- Paas Easter Egg Dye
- Turmeric Spice
- Cochineal
- Pulverized Clay
- Indigo
- Logwood
- Madder
- Cutch

MORDANTS:

In general, mordants are metallic salts, which induce colour peculiar to the metal, from which the salt is extracted. You may wish to experiment by mixing mordants to achieve unusual results.

TIN: (stannous chloride), makes bright colours

ALUM: (aluminum potassium), it gives best results when used before wool is dyed. Mixed with dye bath.

CHROME: (potassium dichromate/bichromate), makes shades of rust, golds, brasses, and blue. Use before dye. **Chrome is highly poisonous avoid inhaling fumes.**

COPPER SULPHATE: (blue vitriol or bluestone) makes greenish tones to the colours for wool fibres.

COPPERAS: (ferrous sulfate), produces purples, black and green from certain dye stuff.

CREAM OF TARTAR: (tartaric acid), is a standard substance used for dyeing wool. It is used to make bright colours, mixed while wool is dyeing.

LEVELING AGENTS: these are salts that are used to level dye pots when desiring slightly dulled colours. Submerge dyed wool in warm water, simmer for thirty minutes to one hour on the shade of colour you desire.

LINCHENS: These are featherly fronds hanging from mature trees containing their own acid, therefore, no need of mordanting is required.

MEASUREMENTS OF MORDANT:

ALUM:	4oz (113 gr) to	16 oz (454 gr) of wool
TIN:	¼ oz (7gr) to	16 oz (454 gr) of wool
CHROME:	½ oz (14 gr) to	16 oz (454 gr) of wool
COPPERAS:	½ oz (14 gr) to	16 oz (454 gr) of wool
COPPER SULPHATE:	1oz (29 gr) to	16 oz (454 gr) of wool
CREAM OF TARTAR:	1 oz (29 gr) to	16 oz (454 gr) of wool

CUSTOM WOOL DYEING:

RAW DYE STUFF	MORDANT(S)	PROBABLE COLOURS
Acorn nut and cups	Alum	Tan
Acorn nut and cups	Alum with Oxalic Acid	Yellow-Tan
Acorn nut and cups	Tin with Oxalic Acid	Yellow-Tan
Ageratum	Alum	Light Yellow
Ageratum	Tin	Bright Yellow
*Alfalfa	Tin & Copper	Green-gold
Alfalfa	Alum	Cream
Alfalfa	Tin	Pale-Yellow
Alder bark	Alum	Soft Brown
Apple bark	Alum	Lemon Yellow
Apple bark	Tin	Bright Yellow
Apple bark	Chrome	Brass
Apple bark	Alum, Copper & Oxalic Acid	Dark Brown
Apple bark	Alum & Ammonia	Yellow
Apple bark	Tin & Copper Sulfate	Old Gold
Asparagus plant (fall)	Tin	Yellow
Aster, wild (white)	Alum	Yellow
Aster, wild (white)	Chrome	Gold
Aster (purple)	Tin	Soft Yellow
Barberries	Alum	Yellow-Gold to Coral
Barberries	Tin & Copper Sulfate	Light Khaki
Barberry stem or root	Alum	Yellow
Barberry stem or root	Tin	Deep Yellow
Bayberry leaves & berries	Alum	Gray-Green to Light Yellow
Bayberry leaves & berries	Tin	Light Yellow
Bayberry leaves & berries	Copper	Dark Brown
Black Tea	---	Shade Colour
Barley tobacco	Alum	Tobacco Brown
Black Walnut	Alum	Shade of Brown
Beets (whole plant)	---	Red, Browns
Beets (whole plant)	Alum	Tan to Red-Orange
Beets (whole plant)	Tin	Gold to Yellow-Orange
Beets (whole plant)	Tin & Copper Sulfate	Dark Yellow-Green

RAW DYE STUFF	MORDANT(S)	PROBABLE COLOURS
Birch leaves	Alum	Green-Yellow to Tan
Birch leaves	Tin	Yellow
Bittersweet berries	Alum	Light Tan
Bittersweet berries	Tin	Bright Orange-Yellow
Bittersweet berries	Tin & Oxalic Acid	Pink-Tan
Blackberries	Alum	Purple with Brown tones
Blackberries	Alum & Salt	Blue-Gray
Blackberry shoots	Copper	Black
Black eyed-susan (blossom)	Alum	Grayed-Yellow
Black eyes-susan (blossom)	Tin & Copper & Oxalic Acid	Medium Brown
Bloodroot	---	Orange
Bloodroot	Alum or Tin	Reds or Pinks
Broom, (scotch)	Alum	Yellow
Broom, (scotch)	Chrome	Gold
Broom sedge	Alum	Green-Yellow
Broom sedge	Chrome	Brass
Buck brush berries	Tin	Light Yellow
Buck brush berries	Alum & Ammonia	Soft Yellow
Buck brush berries	Tin & Ammonia	Yellow
Buckthorn bark	Alum	Golden Yellow
Buckthorn bark	Tin	Orange-Brown
Buckthorn bark	Alum & Ammonia	Gold
Buckthorn bark	Tin & Ammonia	Bright Gold
Buckthorn bark	Alum & Oxalic Acid	Deep Rose-Tan
Buckthorn bark	Tin & Oxalic Acid	Dark Brown
Buttercups	Alum	Yellow
Butternut hulls	Alum	Dull Red-Orange
Butternut hulls	Tin	Dull Yellow-Orange
Butternut hulls	Alum & Ammonia	Pink-Beige
Butternut hulls	Tin & Ammonia	Gray-Brown
Butternut hulls	Alum or Tin & Oxalic Acid	Bright Orange- Brown
Butternut hulls	Alum & Copper	Medium Brown
Calliopsis	Chrome	Bright Red
Chamomile (blossoms)	Alum	Buff

RAW DYE STUFF	MORDANT(S)	PROBABLE COLOURS
Chamomile (golden marguerites)	Chrome	Gold
Canna leaves and stems (autumn)	Alum	Yellow-Tan
Canna leaves and stems (autumn)	Tin	Gray-Yellow
Canna leaves and stems (autumn)	Alum or Tin & Ammonia	Yellow
Canna leaves and stems (autumn)	Tin or Alum & Oxalic Acid	Grayed Red-Orange
Carrion (berries & leaves autumn)	Alum & Oxalic Acid	Light Yellow-Orange
Coffee	Alum	Coffee colour
Crab Apples	Tin	Ruby, Carmine Red
Carrot tops	---	Gold, Yellow
Carrot tops	Alum	Light Green-Yellow
Carrot tops	Tin	Bright Yellow
Carrot tops	Alum & Ammonia	Bright Yellow
Carrot tops	Tin & Ammonia	Blue
Catnip (autumn)	Alum	Light Yellow
Catnip (autumn)	Tin	Gray-Yellow
Catnip (autumn)	Tin & Oxalic Acid	Gray-Gold
Cedar roots	Alum	Purple
Cherry bark	Alum	Pale Rose
Cherry bark	Tin	Peach
Cherry bark	Alum & Oxalic Acid	Light Red-Orange
Cherry bark	Alum & Copper Sulfate	Olive Green
Cherry Wood	Alum	Tan
Cherry Wood	Tin	Bright Gold
Cherry Wood	Copper & Alum & Oxalic Acid	Dark Brown
Cherry Wood	Alum or Tin & Oxalic Acid	Light Grayed Red-Orange
Cherry Wood	Alum or Tin & Ammonia	Light Red-Orange
Cherry Wood	Alum & Copper Sulfate	Olive Green
Cherry Wood	Tin or Alum & Copper Sulfate	---

RAW DYE STUFF	MORDANT(S)	PROBABLE COLOURS
Cherry Wood	Oxalic Acid	Red-Gold
Chestnut bark	Alum	Brown
Chestnut bark	Copper	Warm Gray
Chestnut (leaves & hulls)	Chrome	Gold
Choke cherry (root, leaves)	---	Purple-Brown
Choke cherry (fruit)	Alum	Red
Chrysanthemum (blossoms, yellow)	Tin	Yellow
Chrysanthemum (blossoms, red)	Tin	Bronze
Chrysanthemum (blossoms, red)	Alum & Ammonia	Light Yellow
Chrysanthemum (blossoms, red)	Tin & Ammonia	Lime Green
Chrysanthemum (blossoms, red)	Alum & Oxalic Acid	Red-Violet
Chrysanthemum (blossoms, red)	Tin & Oxalic Acid	Deep Red-Violet
Clematis (leaves & branches)	Alum	Yellow
Cochineal	-----	Rose Pink
Cochineal	Acids	Orange
Cochineal	Alkalis	Crimson Violet
Cochineal	Alum	Red, Rose, Pinks
Cochineal	Tin	Orange-Red
Cochineal	Copper	Deep Red-Violet
Cochineal	Copper Sulfate	Red-Violet
Cochineal	Chrome & Acetic Acid	Purple
Cochineal	Oxalic Acid	Geranium Red
Cocklebur	Alum	Gold
Cocklebur	Tin & Ammonia	Yellow
Cocklebur	Chrome	Brown
Cocklebur	Tin & Oxalic Acid	Gold
Cocklebur	Copper	Dark Green
Coleus (purple)	Alum	Gray-Brown
Coleus (purple)	Tin	Green-Brown
Coleus (purple)	Alum & Ammonia	Olive Green
Coleus (purple)	Alum & Oxalic Acid	Rose
Coleus (purple)	Tin & Oxalic Acid	Medium Gray-Brown
Coleus (green & pink)	Alum & Tin	Yellow-Tan

RAW DYE STUFF	MORDANT(S)	PROBABLE COLOURS
Coleus (green & pink)	Alum & Oxalic Acid	Grayed Red-Orange
Coleus (green & pink)	Tin & Oxalic Acid	Medium Brown
Kool-Aid (unsweetened)	----	Yellows, Greens
Coreopsis (blossoms & leaves)	Tin	Bright Yellow
Coreopsis (blossoms & leaves)	Chrome	Burnt Orange
Coreopsis (stalk)	Alum	Light Yellow
Cranberry	Alum	Pink
Cranberry	Tin	Red-Gold
Cranberry	Alum & Oxalic Acid	----
Cranberry	Tin & Oxalic Acid	Light Red-Violet
Cranberry	Alum & Ammonia	Grayed Pink
Cranberry	Tin & Ammonia	Dull Gold
Curry Powder	Alum	Bright Gold
Curry Powder	Tin	Bright-Orange
Dahlia (blossom)	Alum	Yellow
Dahlia (blossom)	Chrome	Orange
Dahlia (leaves, autumn)	Tin	Grayed Gold
Dahlia (leaves, autumn)	Alum & Oxalic Acid	Dark Tan
Dahlia (leaves, autumn)	Copper & Alum & Ammonia	Warm Gray
Dahlia (leaves, autumn)	Copper & Tin & Ammonia	Yellow-Brown
Dandelion (blossoms)	Alum	Soft Yellow
Dandelion (blossoms)	Tin	Brighter Yellows
Dock, broad leaved	Alum	Yellow
Dock, broad leaved (roots)	Alum	Dull Yellow
Dock, broad leaved (roots)	Chrome	Light Brown
Elderberries	Chrome	Greenish Blue
Fennel plant	Alum	Bright Yellow
Fennel plant	Chrome	Gold
Fern, bracken	Alum	Lime Green
Fern shoots	Copper	Dull Green
Fern, sweet (summer time)	Tin	Golden Yellow
Fern, sweet (summer time)	Alum or Tin & Oxalic Acid	Light Red-Orange
Geranium (blossoms)	Tin	Pink
Gloxinia (blossoms, red)	Alum or Tin & Oxalic Acid	Deep Pink

RAW DYE STUFF	MORDANT(S)	PROBABLE COLOURS
Gloxinia (blossoms, red)	Alum	Pale Pink
Gloxinia (blossoms, red)	Tin	Grayed yellow
Goldenrod (blossoms)	Alum	Yellow
Grapes (purple)	Alum	Purple with Brown Tones
Grapes (wild)	Alum	Lavender to Violet
Hawthorn apples	Alum	Deep Fawn
Hickory (twigs or leaves)	Alum	Shades of Tan
Hickory (nut hulls)	Alum	Deep Red-Orange
Hickory (nut hulls)	Tin	Orange
Hickory (nut hulls)	Alum or Tin & Oxalic Acid	Deep Red-Orange
Hollyhock (mixed)	Chrome	Orange and Rust
Hollyhock (red)	Alum	Pink
Hollyhock (red)	Tin	Deep Red
Hop wild (leaves & flowers)	Alum	Yellow
Hop, wild (stalks)	Alum	Brown Red
Horn bean (inner bark)	----	Yellow
Horse brier fruit	Alum	Violet
Horse brier fruit	Table Salt	Blue
Horsetail stalks	Alum	Grayed Yellow
Huckleberries	Alum	Violet
Huckleberries	Tin	Blue
Huckleberries	Alum & Ammonia	Light Blue-Green
Huckleberries	Tin & Ammonia	Deep Green
Huckleberries	Alum & Oxalic Acid	Violet
Huckleberries	Tin & Oxalic Acid	Deep Blue
Huckleberries	Copper & Tin & Ammonia	Dark Green
Indigo (roots or powder)	Alum	Blue
Indigo (roots or powder)	Chrome	Green
Indigo with turmeric	Alum	Light Green
Iris	Alum or Tin	Yellows, Blues & Greens
Iris	Chrome	Green
Ironweed	Alum	Tan
Juniper berries	Alum	Yellow
Juniper berries	Copper Sulfate & Ammonia	Olive Brown

RAW DYE STUFF	MORDANT(S)	PROBABLE COLOURS
Juniper berries	Copper	Brown
Knotweed	Alum	Pale Yellow
Knotweed	Tin	Yellow
Knotweed	Alum & Oxalic Acid	Pink
Knotweed	Tin & Oxalic Acid	Peach
Lamb's quarters	-----	Red
Larch needles (fresh)	Alum	Brown
Larkspur (blossoms)	Alum	Blue
Larkspur (plant)	Alum or Tin	Grayed Tan
Larkspur (plant)	Alum or Tin & Oxalic Acid	Medium Brown
Lichens	----	Plum
Lichens	Alum or Tin	Grayed Red-Orange
Lichens	Coppers	Brown (lighter)
Lichens	Alum (double dose)	Shades of Brown and Yellows
Lichens	Copper & Tin & Ammonia	Medium Brown
Lichens (parmelia molluscula)	Alum	Red-Tan to light Orange
Lichens (peltigera)	Alum	Yellow Tan
Lichens (usnea)	Alum	Buff to Green-Yellow
Lichens (umbilicaria pustilata)	Soaked in Ammonia	Deep Red-Violet
Lilac (branches & leaves)	Alum	Medium Yellow
Lilac (branches & leaves)	Tin	Medium Yellow
Lilac (branches & leaves)	Chrome & Oxalic Acid	Warm Gray
Lilac (branches & leaves)	Copper Sulfate & Alum & Oxalic Acid	Gold
Lilac (branches & leaves)	Copper Sulfate & Tin	Olive Green
Lilly of the Valley (spring time)	Alum	Yellow Green
Lilly of the Valley (spring time)	Alum & Lime	Yellowish Green
Lilly of the Valley (spring time)	Alum & Ammonia	Greenish Yellow
Lilly of the Valley (fall time)	Alum	Peach
Lilly of the Valley (fall time)	Tin	Red Orange
Lilly of the Valley (fall time)	Alum & Oxalic Acid	Grayed Brown
Locust Seed Pods (dark brown)	Alum	Tan
Locust Seed Pods (dark brown)	Alum & Ammonia	Grayed Yellow-Orange
Locust Seed Pods (dark brown)	Tin	Bright Orange
Locust Seed Pods (dark brown)	Copper & Alum & Ammonia	Dark Gray

RAW DYE STUFF	MORDANT(S)	PROBABLE COLOURS
Locust Seed Pods (dark brown)	Copper & Tin & Ammonia	Deep Bronze
Locust Seed Pods (dark brown)	Copper & Alum & Oxalic Acid	Warm Light Gray
Locust Seed Pods (dark brown)	Copper & Tin & Oxalic Acid	Gold
Locust Seed Pods (rust)	Alum	Pale Peach
Locust Seed Pods (rust)	Tin	Clear Yellow
Locust Seed Pods (rust)	Alum & Ammonia	Grayed Yellow
Locust Seed Pods (rust)	Tin & Ammonia	Yellow-Orange
Locust Seed Pods (rust)	Alum & Oxalic Acid	Pale Peach
Locust Seed Pods (rust)	Tin & Oxalic Acid	Light Red-Orange
Locust Yellow	Alum	Yellow
Logwood	----	Range of Blues
Logwood	Coppers	Dark Blue with Gray
Logwood	Chrome	Black
Madder Roots	Chrome	Yellow
Madder Roots	Alum	Bright Red-Orange
Madder Roots	Tin	Bright Orange
Madder Roots	Alum & Ammonia	Light Yellow
Madder Roots	Tin & Ammonia	Clear Yellow
Madder Roots	Alum & Oxalic Acid	Bright Rust
Madder Roots with Yellow Onion Skins	Alum	Orange
Maple bark	Alum	Pink-Tan
Marigold	Alum	Yellow, lighter shades
Marigold (French) Plants & Blossoms	Alum	Lemon Yellow
Marigold (French) Plants & Blossoms	Tin	Bright Orange
Marigold (French) Plants & Blossoms	Alum & Ammonia	Yellow
Marigold (French) Plants & Blossoms	Tin & Ammonia	Yellow Orange
Marigold (French) Plants & Blossoms	Alum & Oxalic Acid	Tan
Marigold (French) Plants & Blossoms	Tin & Oxalic Acid	Yellow

RAW DYE STUFF	MORDANT(S)	PROBABLE COLOURS
Marigold (French) Plants & Blossoms	Alum & Copper	Grayed Olive
Marigold (French) Plants & Blossoms	Copper & Tin	Orange Brown
Marigold (American) Plant & Blossoms	Alum	Yellow
Marigold (American) Plant & Blossoms	Tin	Yellow-Green
Marigold (American) Plant & Blossoms	Chrome	Orange
Marigold, marsh (blossoms)	Alum	Orange
Mulberry	Alum	Purple
Mulberry	Oxalic Acid	Pink
Mulberry	Ammonia	Blue
Nectarine (leaves Fall time)	Alum	Lemon Yellow
Nectarine (leaves Fall time)	Tin	Bright Yellow-Orange
Nectarine (leaves Fall time)	Alum & Ammonia	Light Yellow
Nectarine (leaves Fall time)	Copper & Alum & Ammonia	Bronze
Nectarine (leaves Fall time)	Copper & Tin & Ammonia	Orange-Brown
Nettle (flowers)	Alum	Dull Gold
Nettle (whole plant)	Alum	Yellow
Nightshade (berries)	Alum	Purple
Nightshade (berries)	Tin	Blue
Oak, black (bark)	Alum	Yellow
Oak, black (bark)	Chrome	Gold
Oak, black (galls or gallnuts)	----	Brown
Onion Skins (yellow or red)	Tin	Dark, Yellow, Gold, Brasses
Onion Skins (yellow or red)	Alum	Orange
Onion Skins (yellow or red)	Chrome	Red to Brass
Onion Skins (yellow or red)	Tin or Alum & Oxalic Acid	Red-Orange
Onion Skins (yellow or red)	Alum & Ammonia	Gold
Onion Skins (yellow or red)	Tin & Ammonia	Green-Gold
Onion Skins (yellow or red)	Copper Sulfate	Yellow-Green

RAW DYE STUFF	MORDANT(S)	PROBABLE COLOURS
Oregon Grape (roots, leaves, stems)	Alum	Dull Yellow-Green
Osage orange (bark, wood chips)	Alum	Yellow-Green
Osage orange (bark, wood chips)	Tin	Yellow-Gold
Osage orange (bark, wood chips)	Chrome	Gold
Oxalis (foliage, Fall time)	Alum	Light Peach
Oxalis (foliage, Fall time)	Tin	Grayed Red-Orange
Oxalis (foliage, Fall time)	Alum & Ammonia	Light Yellow
Oxalis (foliage, Fall time)	Tin & Ammonia	Clear Yellow
Oxalis (foliage, Fall time)	Alum & Copper & Ammonia	Gold
Paprika	Alum	Tan
Pear (sawdust or wood chips)	Alum	Peach
Pear (sawdust or wood chips)	Tin	Rose
Pear (sawdust or wood chips)	Alum & Ammonia	Red-Orange
Pear (sawdust or wood chips)	Tin & Ammonia	Dusty-Rose
Pear (sawdust or wood chips)	Alum or Tin & Oxalic Acid	Red-Orange
Pear (sawdust or wood chips)	Copper & Alum & Ammonia	Warm Gray
Pear (sawdust or wood chips)	Copper & Tin & Ammonia	Cool Gray
Pear (sawdust or wood chips)	Alum & Copper Sulfate & Ammonia	Grayed Green
Peony (blossoms red, pink)	Alum	Yellow
Peony (blossoms red, pink)	Alum & Oxalic Acid	Red and Pink
Pine Cones (extensive boiling)	Alum	Dull Brown-Yellow
Pine Cones (extensive boiling)	Alum & Oxalic Acid	Rose Tan
Pine Needles (fresh)	Alum	Olive Green
Plantain (leaves, roots)	Alum	Green
Plum, Damsons (fruit)	Alum	Gray
Plum, wild (roots)	Alum	Red-Purple
Plum, wild (bark)	Alum	Red

RAW DYE STUFF	MORDANT(S)	PROBABLE COLOURS
Pokeberry	Alum	Red & Pink
Pokeberry	Chrome	Rust
Pokeberry	Tin	Bright Red
Polyporus lucidus (red shell fungi) or lichens	Alum	Pale Purple
Polyporus lucidus (red shell fungi) or lichens	Tin	Pale Red-Orange
Polyporus lucidus (red shell fungi) or lichens	Alum or Tin & Oxalic Acid	Bright Orange
Polyporus lucidus (red shell fungi) or lichens	Copper & Alum & Oxalic Acid	Deep Brown
Pomegranate skins	Alum	Yellow
Pomegranate skins	Copper & Ash Lye	Violet-Blue
Poplar (leaves)	Alum	Lime Yellow
Poplar (bark)	Alum	Rich Yellow
Poppy, oriental (petals)	Alum & Oxalic Acid	Salmon Pink
Poppy oriental (stems only)	Alum & Oxalic Acid	Violet
Privet (berries)	Alum & Salt	Blue
Privet (clippings)	Alum	Tan
Privet (clippings)	Tin	Deep Gold
Privet (clippings)	Copper Sulfate	Green
Privet (clippings)	Copper & Tin & Ammonia	Golden Brown
Privet (clippings)	Chrome	Tan to Gold
Privet or Ironwood (berries)	Alum	Tan
Privet or Ironwood (berries)	Tin	Dark Brown
Privet or Ironwood (berries)	Alum & Ammonia	Grayed Gold
Privet or Ironwood (berries)	Tin & Ammonia	Brass
Privet or Ironwood (berries)	Alum & Oxalic Acid	Dusty Rose
Privet or Ironwood (berries)	Tin & Oxalic Acid	Dark Grayed Brown
Privet or Ironwood (berries)	Copper & Alum	Dark Grayed Green

RAW DYE STUFF	MORDANT(S)	PROBABLE COLOURS
Privet or Ironwood (berries)	Copper & Tin	Dark Grayed Brown
Purple Indian corn	Alum	Shades of Purple
Purslane	Alum	Beige
Ragweed (young)	Alum	Green
Ragweed (young)	Alum & Copper	Dark Green
Red Cedar Twigs	Chrome	Red-Browns
Red beans (dry)	Chrome	Red-Browns
Red Onion Skins	Chrome	Dark Gold
Rose Bush (wild fall time)	Alum	Gray to Brown
Rose Bush (cuttings)	Alum	Tan
Rose Bush (cuttings)	Copper	Green to Brown Black
Rose Hips	Alum	Grayed Rose
Rose Hips	Tin	Gold
Rudbeckia (flower heads)	Alum	Green
Rudbeckia (flower heads)	Chrome	Green Gold
Saffron (flowers or powder)	Alum	Yellow
Salvia (plant with blossoms fall time)	Alum or Tin	Pale Yellow
Salvia (plant with blossoms fall time)	Tin & Ammonia	Grayed Gold
Salvia (plant with blossoms fall time)	Alum or Tin & Oxalic Acid	Peach
Salvia (plant with blossoms fall time)	Copper & Alum & Ammonia	Cool Gray
Salvia (plant with blossoms fall time)	Copper & Tin & Ammonia	Grayed Gold
Salvia (plant with blossoms fall time)	Copper & Alum & Oxalic Acid	Green
Salvia (plant with blossoms fall time)	Copper & Tin & Oxalic Acid	Grayed Gold
Scabiosa (blossoms)	Alum	Bright Yellow-Green
Scabiosa (blossoms)	Tin	Yellow Green
Scabiosa (blossoms)	Alum & Ammonia	Clear Yellow
Scabiosa (blossoms)	Tin & Ammonia	Green-Yellow

RAW DYE STUFF	MORDANT(S)	PROBABLE COLOURS
Scabiosa (blossoms)	Alum & Oxalic Acid	Dusty Rose
Scabiosa (blossoms)	Tin & Oxalic Acid	Grayed Rose
Scabiosa (blossoms)	Copper & Alum	Dark Yellow-Green
Scabiosa (blossoms)	Copper & Tin	Grayed Gold
Scabiosa (whole plant)	Tin	Clear Yellow
Scabiosa (whole plant)	Alum & Ammonia	Grayed Yellow
Scabiosa (whole plant)	Tin & Ammonia	Golden Yellow
Scabiosa (whole plant)	Copper & Alum & Ammonia	Grayed Olive Green
Scabiosa (whole plant)	Copper & Tin & Ammonia	Yellow-Brown
Seaweed (spring time)	Alum	Light Tan
Seaweed (spring time)	Coppers	Yellow Green
Seaweed (spring time)	Alum & Ammonia	Yellow Fawn
Seaweed (spring time)	Tin & Ammonia	Red-Brown
Sedge Grass	Alum	Yellow-Green to Tan
Sedge Grass	Chrome	Gold
Sedge Grass	Copper	Gray Green
Sheep's sorrel	Alum	Soft Pink
Sheep's sorrel	Copper	Mushroom Pink
Smartweed	Alum	Yellow-Green
Solomon seal (leaves)	Alum	Green
Spiderwort (blossoms)	Alum	Blue
Sumac (leaves & berries)	Alum	Tan
Sumac (leaves & berries)	Copper Sulfate	Green
Sumac (leaves & berries)	Copper	Gray or Gray Brown
Sunflower Seeds	Alum	Yellowish Tan
Sycamore (fruit)	Alum	Gray Yellow
Tansy (flower heads)	Alum	Green Yellow
Tansy (flower heads)	Tin	Brown
Thistle, (Russian, whole young plant)	Wool & plant soak together one week while plant ferments	dull olive green
Thyme foliage (fall)	Alum	Grayed Gold
Thyme foliage (fall)	Tin	Yellow
Thyme foliage (fall)	Alum & Ammonia	Brass

RAW DYE STUFF	MORDANT(S)	PROBABLE COLOURS
Thyme foliage (fall)	Tin & Ammonia	Gold
Thyme foliage (fall)	Alum & Oxalic Acid	Grayed Red-Orange
Thyme foliage (fall)	Tin & Oxalic Acid	Yellow Brown
Thyme foliage (fall)	Copper & Alum	Bronze
Thyme foliage (fall)	Copper & Tin	Grayed Red-Orange
Thyme foliage (fall)	Alum & Oxalic Acid	Yellow-Brown
Thyme foliage (fall)	Tin & Oxalic Acid	Yellow Brown
Thyme foliage (fall)	Copper & Alum	Bronze
Thyme foliage (fall)	Copper & Tin	Grayed Red-Orange
Tomato plant (before frost)	Alum & Ammonia	Grayed Yellow
Tomato plant (before frost)	Tin & Ammonia	Grayed Golden Yellow
Tomato plant (before frost)	Tin	Clear Yellow
Tomato plant (before frost)	Alum	Shades of Tan
Tomato plant (before frost)	Copper & Alum	Cool Gray
Tomato plant (before frost)	Copper & Tin	Deep Yellow
Tulip petals	Alum	Beige and Yellow
Tulip petals	Oxalic Acid	Deep Yellow
Tulip tree (leaves)	Chrome	Gold
Turmeric	Alum	Yellow
Turmeric	Copper Sulfate	Green
Wahoo (berries, fall time)	Alum	Pale Yellow-Orange
Wahoo (berries, fall time)	Tin	Deep Yellow-Orange
Wahoo (berries, fall time)	Alum & Ammonia	Golden Yellow
Wahoo (berries, fall time)	Copper & Alum & Ammonia	Brass
Wahoo (berries, fall time)	Copper & Tin & Ammonia	Golden Brown
Walnut, black (hulls)	Alum	Brown and Tan
Walnut, black (hulls)	----	Brown
Walnut, black (hulls)	Copper	Black and Gray
Walnut, black (hulls)	Alum & Oxalic Acid	Red Brown
Willow (leaves)	Alum	Yellow
Willow (bark)	Alum or Chrome	Gold to Orange-Red and Brown
Wood-charcoal	Coppers	Black-Gray
Yarrow	Copper	Green

NOTE: Please note that although we have included them in our list, these dyer's helpers are not recommended due to their high level of toxicity.

- **Tin/ stannous chlorite**
- **Chrome/ Potassium dichromate**
- **Copper/Copper Sulfate**
- **Acid of sugar/Oxalic Acid**

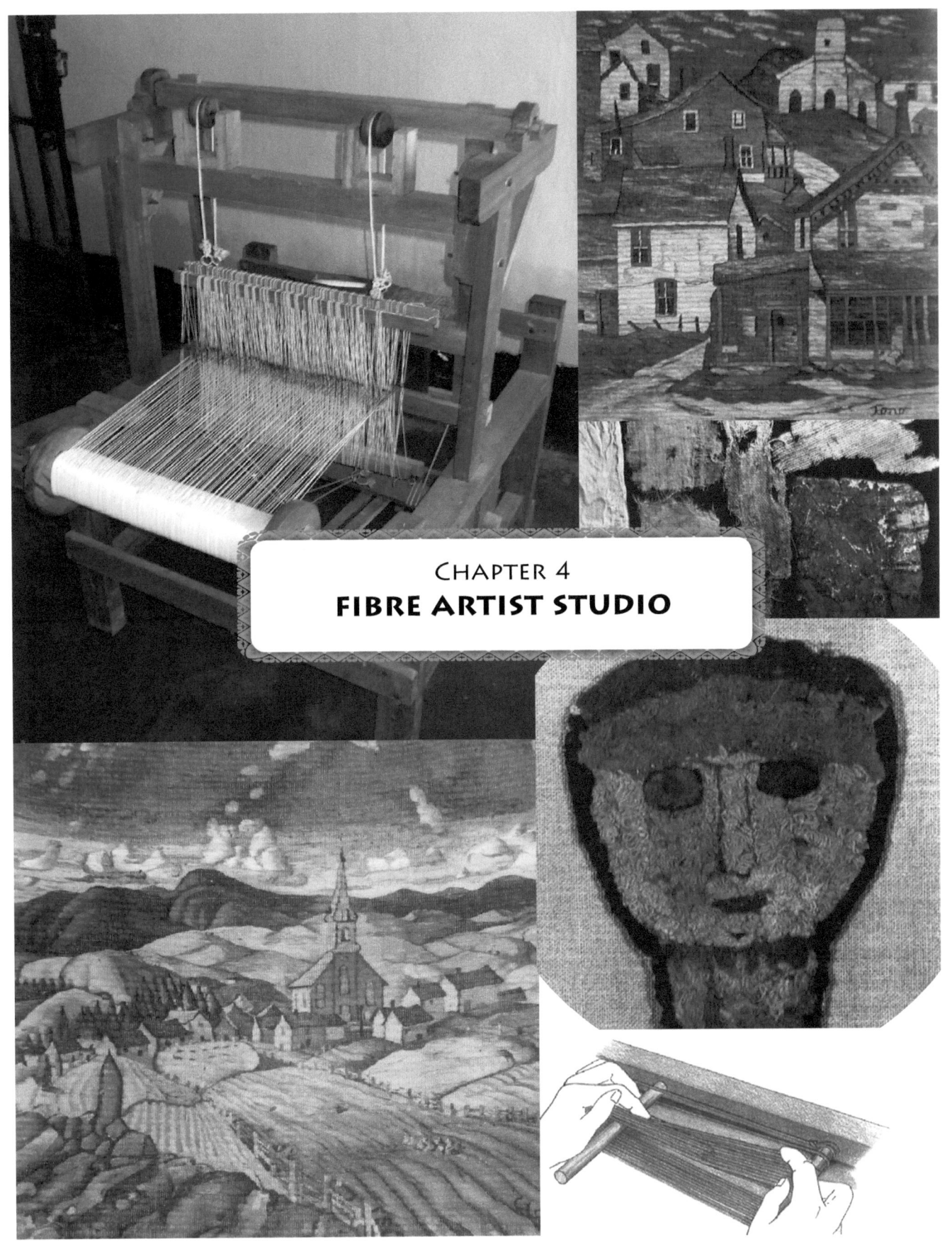

Chapter 4
FIBRE ARTIST STUDIO

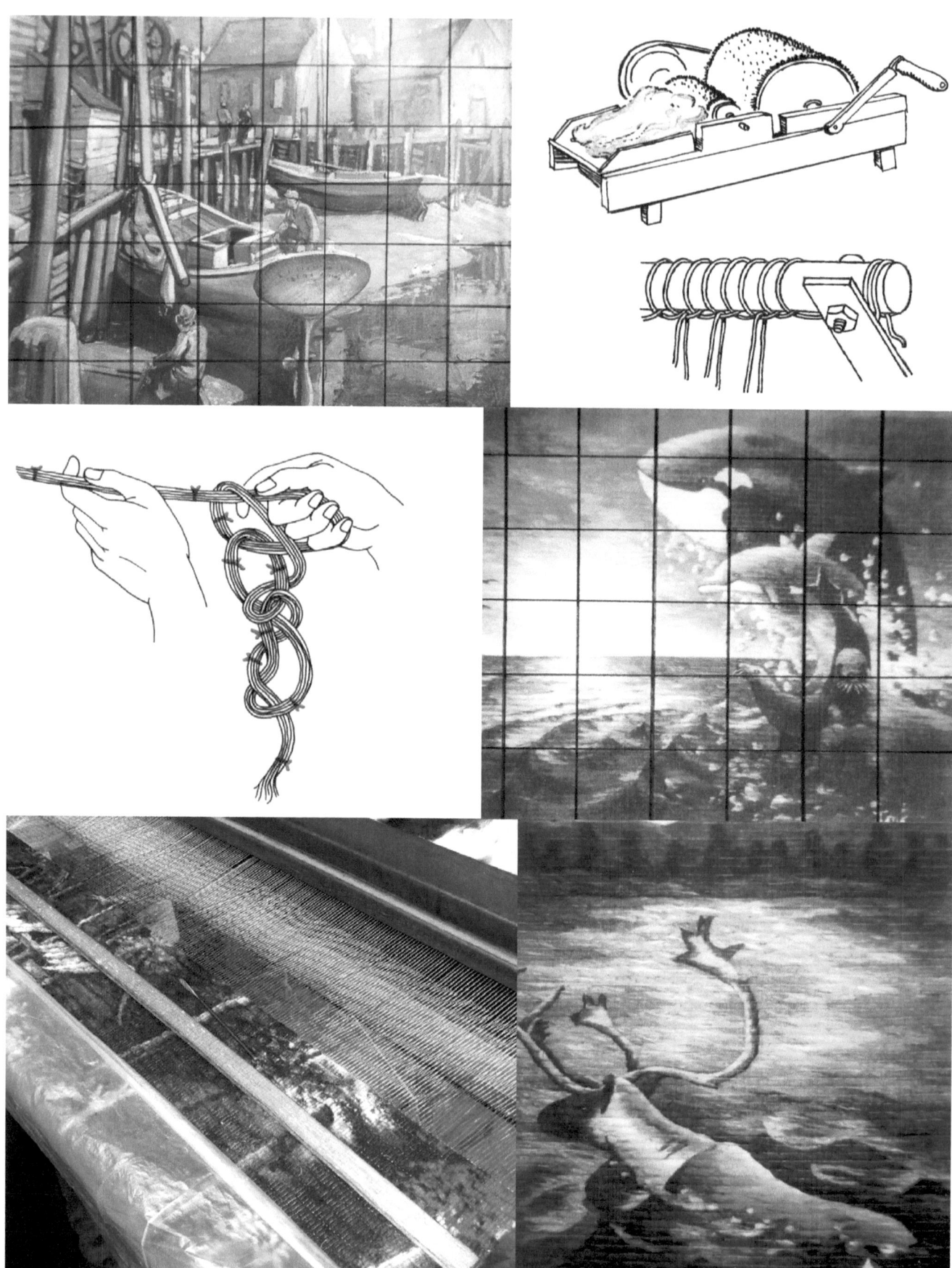

ESSENTIALS OF THE LOOM

Let us begin with the question of what is a loom? The answer is simple. A loom is a device that holds the warp ends, or threads, taut so that a shed or opening, can be formed. Through this shed the weft thread is passed, and the interlocking process between the warp thread, inlaid wool, and weft thread is achieved.

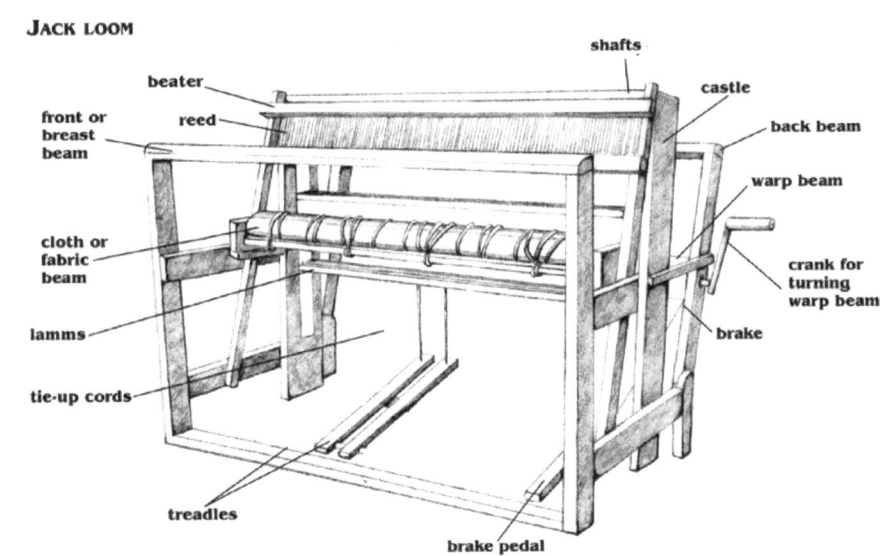

Throughout the centuries of weaving evolution, the types of looms used varied from one geographical area to another. The early Greek weavers seemed to prefer the upright loom, on which one weaves from the top down, as did some North American Indian tribes, and ancient Scandinavians.

Egyptian weavers of about 2500 B.C. used another type of upright, or vertical loom similar to that of the Persian, and also a horizontal loom, such as the type used by the Incas of South America. This latter horizontal loom is still used today in Mexico, Guatemala, and Peru. One thing remains constant: whatever loom was used, the basic principle remained the same (passing and interlocking a weft or horizontal, thread through a stationary warp, or vertical threads).

Today, one can purchase a simple loom or a complex loom. There are rough looms made of tree branches or scrap wood and other more impressive looms made of fine wooden frames available. Whatever the make and style, all looms share something in common: they all must have a shed in order to inlay wool or weft. The way the shed is formed divides all handlooms into three basic types.

The Jack Loom has some of its shaft **raising** the shed while others remain fixed. For the purpose of inlaid wool, the focus is on one or two rising shafts. The opposite takes place with the **counterbalance** loom; the term describes a shaft that **sinks** the shed. On the other hand in a **countermarch** loom one set of thread rises as the other sink.

All the three types of looms mentioned are equally serviceable and the type you decide to purchase becomes a personal choice depending on what you want to weave. For our purpose on inlaid tapestry, a 2-harness **Jack loom** is the best and most economical; the cost of the loom is determined by the materials used in making it, and the number of harnesses. A two-harness loom is much more economical.

SIMPLE FRAMED LOOMS:

These are variations of the same type of loom that have no harness. Instead they have two different shed openings and at least one shed that opens by using a shed stick.

In the vertical loom, the warp faces the weaver in an up and down position. Small tapestries are usually done in this type of loom. Frame looms can be either vertical or horizontal, depending on whether they are attached to leg supports or set on a table.

Frame looms are the slowest to work with, but this does not mean that the results are less impressive. For a beginner of inlaid tapestry frame looms are a convenient and inexpensive instrument to learn the art. Children may also find the frame looms suitable for the length of their arms. For an experienced inlaid tapessier, small portable frame looms may be also suitable in a variety of ways; for teaching workshops where a simple inlaid tapestry can be finished within a certain time, where the beginner can see the results quicker. Transporting frame looms for teaching out of town workshops can have its advantages, especially if you have to transport more than one. Trial and error practice on a small frame loom can be less costly and time consuming before transplanting the idea into the much larger inlaid tapestry.

PARTS FOR FRAME.

In order to communicate with you students and other fibre artists, it is important to have common terms that identify each part of the frame and upright loom. Remember, in the frame and upright looms there are no harnesses, treadles, levers, beaters, or reed.

HEDDLES: are long loops of strings through which the warp passes. The heddles are secured to the heddle rod.

HEDDLE ROD: carries the heddle loops and can be fixed or moveable.

SETT MARKS: marks or scores filed or sawed into the top and bottom frames at 1/8' intervals. They take the place of the reed in the table and floor looms. The warp is spaced between them.

SHED STICK: turning at a right angle makes a shed opening to the warp. It is not attached to the loom.

TENSION STICK: keeps the warp under proper tension for weaving or inlaying wool. It is removed as the warp tightens in the process of inlaying wool or weaving.

TAPESTRY COMB: used to beat the weft. An ordinary comb or fork can do the task well.

WARP END BAR: the warp end revolves around the dowel rod to which are tied the beginning and end of the warp thread. It is placed at the front of the loom.

IN THE FRAME LOOM:

In order to open the shed, the shed stick is turned at a right angle to the warp. Following the inlaying wool, the shuttle carries the weft thread through this opening. To close the shed, return the shed stick to its previous position, and gently set to position the weft thread with a comb or fork. Do not beat the weft, for you will distort the alignment or the inlaid wool design.

Pulling upwards the string heddles makes the next shed opening. This is done one warp thread at a time. As you inlay wool one thread at a time, you begin to insert the weft thread until you reach the end. When you finish the inlaying and weft, the shed is then released, and the weft is gently positioned to maintain the inlaid wool in its right place. This is a slow process of inlaying wool because your hands are doing more than inlaying wool.

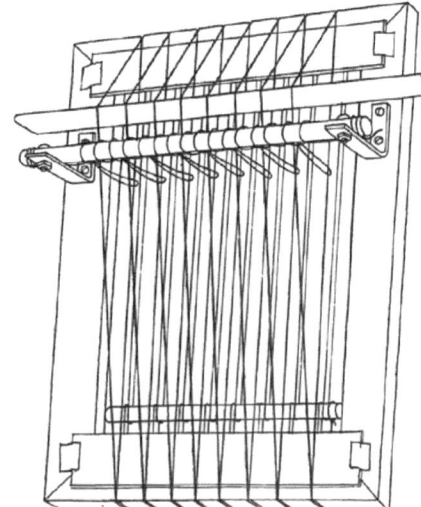

As the tapestry progresses, the shed opening becomes smaller and you may need to remove some of the tension sticks; lift the warp bar so that the inlaid section can be revolved around the bottom towards the back end of the loom.

DRESSING THE FRAME LOOM:

Warping or dressing is made directly on the frame loom. This means that warping ends are put in position as the warp is being wound onto the frame loom. Such, the warp is twice the length of the frame loom, and can be revolved around the frame as the weaving progresses.

Begin by placing a temporary piece of duck tape or fix the warp end bar in some method on the back of the frame loom. This would prevent the bar from shifting at the start of warping.

With a fine marker or pencil mark the positions where the sett marks would begin and end. As you are winding the warp, the ends must be spaced between every ¼" sett mark at the required number of the tapestry's width. For example, if the width of your tapestry is 12" wide your measurement should be 4x12=36 warp threads.

Tension sticks must be taped to the front of the frame loom, both top and bottom. This must be done before warping begins. Those are removed as the work progresses. Even warp tension should always be maintained constant. Just make sure that the ends are not overly tight. On the other hand, should you find tension slacking adjust accordingly.

Wind the warp thread onto a large bobbin. This way you can easily facilitate going around the warp end bar. Unscrew the heddle rod from its base while warping.

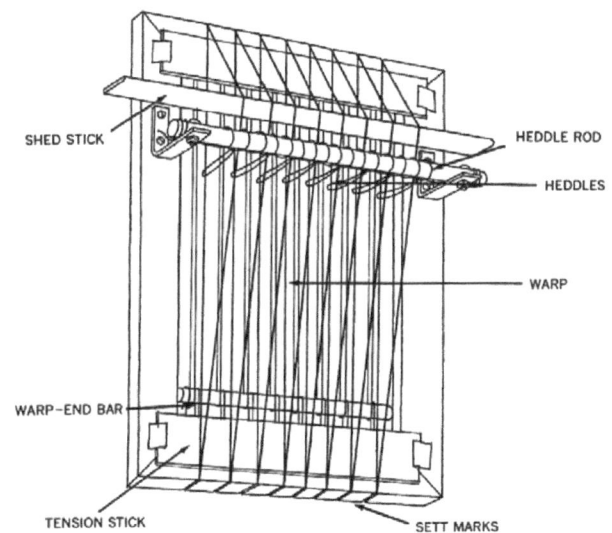

The drawing of the frame loom is showing its underside where the warp end is located. The starting point of the warp is located at the edge of the warp end bar. Take some time to study the drawing before you start to dress the loom. Start by tying the warp thread around the warp end bar. This must be done at the point directly above the sett mark.

Take the warp thread back down and around towards the front side of the loom. Now, go down the front, under the bottom frame, up to the warp end bar, around it and back to the bottom. Warp thread must always be sitting at the sett marks. Follow warping in this way until the required number of warp ends has been placed. The end result should look like the drawing.

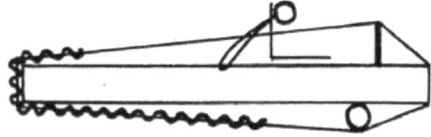

When you tie the last end of the warp thread to the warp end bar, remove the duck tape holding the warp end bar. Re-position the heddle rod. Check that the warp ends are not overly tight. Let us now look at the method that will give you the two shed openings.

TWO SHED SYSTEMS:

To make the first shed use the shed stick. Insert the edge of the stick, back away from the heddle rod, and 'weave' it **under** the **odd** numbered warp thread [that is (1-3-5-7-9-11... and **over** the **even** numbered warp threads (2-4-6-8-10-12...]

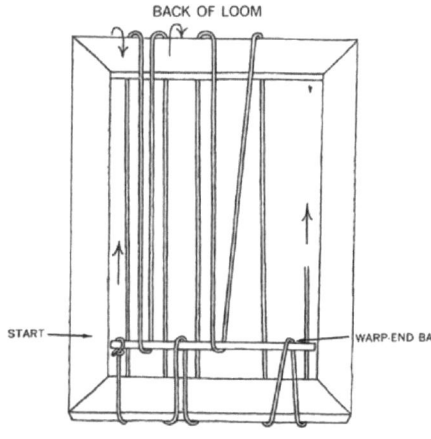

When all the warp threads are wither over or under the shed stick, turn the stick on its edge at the right angle to the warp. Check the arrangements to make sure that the first warp end is **under** (odd numbered ends).
Second Shed heddle loops are made for the second shed. These must be made of strong linen cord; you will also need a blunt edged rug needle.

TO MAKE HEDDLE LOOPS

Take a 2yds of linen cord and tie on to the end of the heddle rod, on the right hand of the loom (or left hand side if you are left handed). Form a half hitch circle over the rod at ½" intervals. Follow the visual direction of the drawing on the heddle bar. Repeat over the entire heddle bar and tie cord around the left hand screw.

Next count the **even** numbered warp ends and cut as many as 10" pieces of linen cord. These 10" pieces of cord are the heddle loops.

Stip the 10" piece of cord **under** the **even** numbered warp ends. Using the rug needle, insert the linen cord into the loop of the heddle cord located just above the warp end you are working with. Tie knot the ends of the cord and the heddle loop is now complete.

When inlaying wool, you can finger lift 2 heddle loops at the time with one hand, while inlaying wool with the other. Remember, as the work progresses the heddle cords may become too short to work with: cut off and replace with new ones.

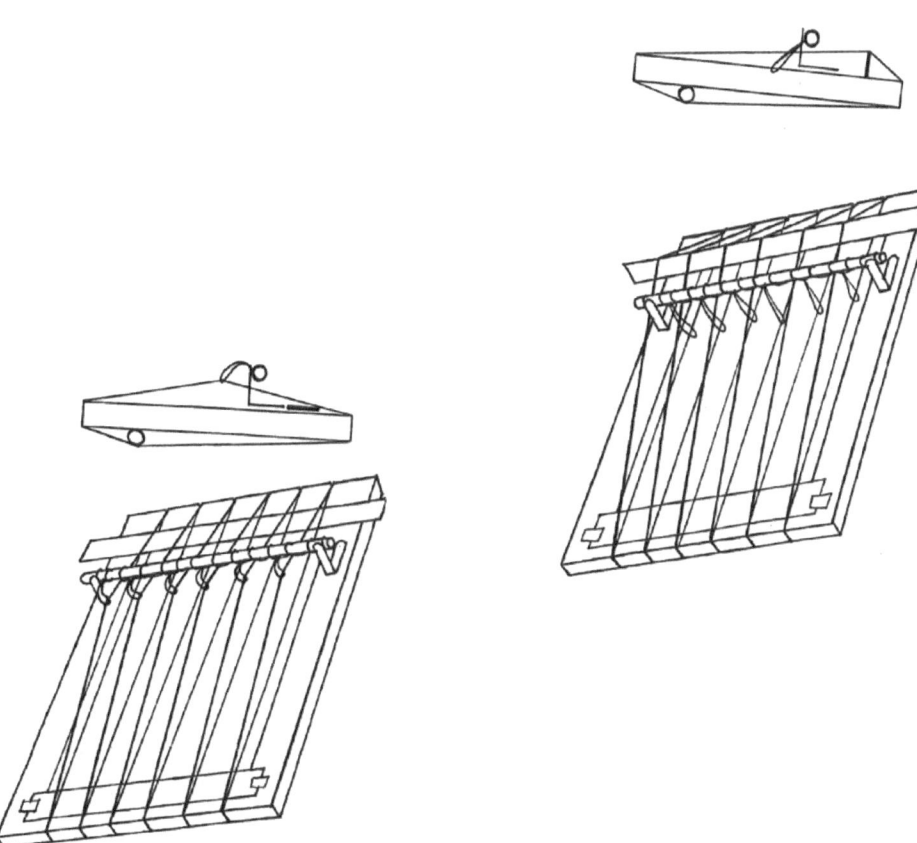

MAKING YOUR OWN FRAME LOOM

Material Needed: The Frame

- 2 pieces ¾" thick, 1¾" wide, 24" long lumber
- 2 pieces ¾" thick, 1¾" wide, 18" long lumber
- 4 (or 8) pieces of flat corner brackets with flat head wood screw.

The Heddle Rod:

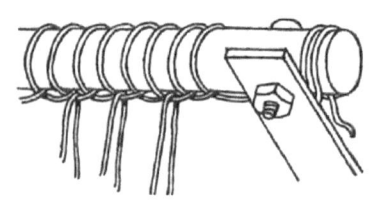

- 2 pieces 2½" metal corner brackets with flat head wood screws
- 1 piece ¾" to 1" diameter wooden dowel (20" long)
- 2 pieces of nut and bolt ¼" diameter.

The Warp End Bar:

- 1 piece of wooden dowel ¾" diameter (18" long)

The Tension Stick:

- 1 flat ½" thick piece of smoothly edged wood 2 ½" wide, 24" long

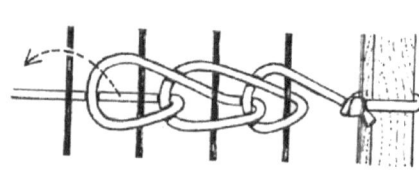

Tools Needed:

Wood Drill, 45 degree saw (hand or electric), screwdriver (adjustable range), wood glue and sandpaper.

BUILDING IT:

- Saw to size the outer frame, and saw its 45 degree corners
- Use a carpenter's square to keep the frame square
- Pour glue on the inside of the 45 degree corners
- Screw flat metal corners as shown in illustration 2

- Saw to size and smooth with sandpaper the heddle rod
- Drill 2 holes 1 ½" from the ends of the heddle rod
- Make sure that the holes are level with the other
- Screw in place the support metal corner brackets of the heddle rod. Follow visual directions.
- The final illustration of how the frame loom is built and how it should look when warped or dressed is in the drawings.

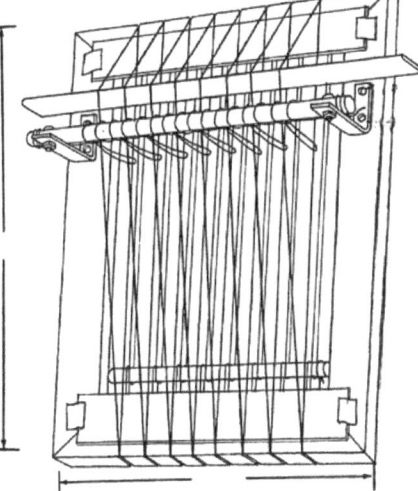

WINDING THE SHUTTLES

Once the loom, whether a frame, table, or floor version is dressed you have only to prepare the weft before inlaid weaving can begin. To do this, the weft thread must be unwound from whatever holds it (a spool, cone, or skin). In small amounts, the thread is put on a shuttle.

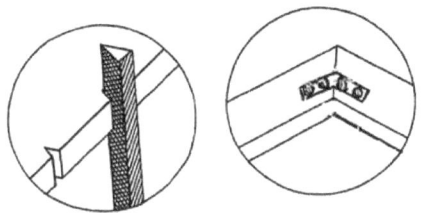

The shuttle is designed to carry the weft thread through the open shed from one side of the loom to the extreme other. Shuttles come in a variety of styles; the one you choose will compliment the width of the shed opening, and the actual weight of the thread. For the frame loom where the shed opening is narrow, the **stick shuttle** is the proper tool.

The stick shuttle is long and flat and is made of lightweight wood or heavy cardboard. Its overall length is from 8" to 18", and is used on frame looms that provide only narrow shed openings. When the stick shuttle is filled, it should resemble the drawings.

Next is the **boat shuttle**. This is also made of wood and is used on looms that allow larger shed openings. Its purpose is made so that it can be thrown from one side of the shed to the other, without touching or brushing either the top or bottom of the shed as the boat shuttle continually passes back and forth.

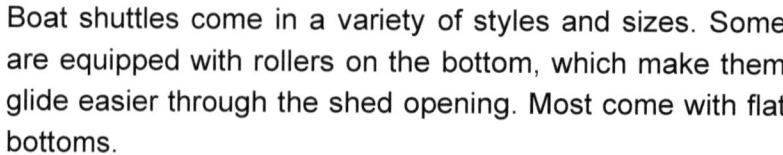

Boat shuttles come in a variety of styles and sizes. Some are equipped with rollers on the bottom, which make them glide easier through the shed opening. Most come with flat bottoms.

Most boat shuttles come with at least one **bobbin.** Choose the one made of plastic, since metal tips cut and can destroy warp edged threads. Standard boat shuttles with bobbins are most popular and can be used for a variety of weave purposes.

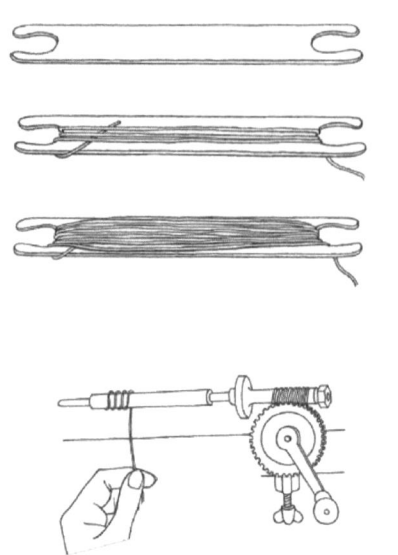

Filling bobbins is usually done either by hand, a slow winding, or by means of electric and hand bobbin winders. You can also use an electric drill or build your own using a small electric motor from a sewing machine or portable mixer.

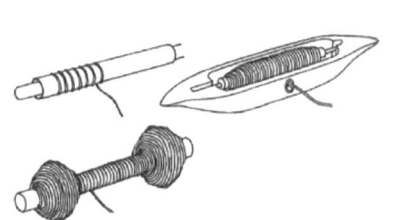

To have a weft thread wound correctly, the two ends of the bobbin are filled up first and the middle last. The reverse would cause the thread not to flow off easily during the process of inlaid weaving. Use alternate thumb pressure to have bobbins tightly wound, for if they are not, the weft thread will roll off at the end of the bobbin and become tangled.

WARPING

Warping is part of the process of dressing the floor loom. The objective is to get the calculated number of warp ends – the individual lengths of pieces of warp – in the correct arrangement, and with equal lengths and tension.

Warping is an essential part of the inlaid pictorial tapestry, thus it must be done well. Some fibre artists find warping tedious work. It requires patience from you and a positive attitude when making a warp. Of course, after repeated processing warps, your co-ordination will become instinctive, relaxing and enjoyable, as inlaid weaving itself.

In order to calculate the number of warps ends needed, you must decide how wide the inlaid tapestry will be, the yarn type, and density of warp ends per inch of sett. To simplify the warp process, the following steps must be taken in sequence:

   a) Choose the warp and weft yarn type.
   b) Calculate the length and width of the warp.
   c) Calculate the overall quantity of the yarn.

The warp yarn type must be sturdy enough to withstand the tension of the loom, the repeated movement of the reed, and the additional weight placed inside the bottom heading plain weave to keep an even tapestry tension, when hanging on the wall.

Cotton linen and nylon yarns are strong enough to serve the purpose of strength and durability. Both warp and weft threads must be of the same colour background matching the pictorial theme.

Several factors will influence the finished tapestry in both length and width other than the warp as it is set. The factors that must be taken into account include **loom_waste, warp take up, shrinkage, and drawn-in.**

The loom waste refers to the need of additional warp length for tying onto the fabric beam and for extending through the reed and heddles at the web of the tapestry.

Warp take-up refers to the extra amount of warp length necessary to go over and under the weft yarns. The extra amount of yarn allowance of 10% is usually enough.

Shrinkage takes place when the loom tension is released. Nearly always shrinkage occurs by the composition of the fibre.

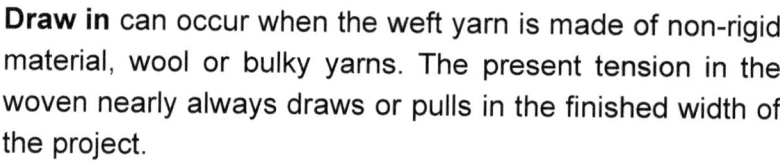

Draw in can occur when the weft yarn is made of non-rigid material, wool or bulky yarns. The present tension in the woven nearly always draws or pulls in the finished width of the project.

To calculate the overall quantity of yarn needed for warping:

a) Determine the width of the pictorial tapestry
b) Add 10% allowance for draw in (for the headings)
c) Add 10% for shrinkage
d) Warp a guide thread on the warping frame to determine the single length of a warp end.

Once you have established the length and width of the warp, you must turn your attention to **determining the_number of warp threads you will need.** This will be pre-determined by the yarn type and by the density of the weave.

For example:

1) Warp the warp thread around a ruler showing inches or centimetres.

2) Lay the thread at 1/8" space between threads. This will be counted at 8 turns per inch.
3) Multiply by the total width inches to determine the number of warp threads you need.
4) Multiply this number with the length of the guide thread on the warping frame (see above #) to establish the overall quantity of warping thread needed.
5) Place the heddles in correct position to hold the warp in identical space sequence.

Now you must calculate the total quantity of warp and weft needed: assuming that the tapestry is 36" in width by 36" in length.

a) At 8 warp threads per inch x 36 inches=228 warp threads
b) Length of each warp = 12 yards x 228=3.456 yards
c) Plus 20% allowance 691.2 yards = 4.147.2 yards.

The above numbers provide only an example. You must make adjustments accordingly. Note that the number of warp threads per inch holds true. Change in the width and length of the above example would alter the above calculations.

Calculating quantity of weft yarn for pictorial tapestry, you need to take into account the weaving of the heading. A heading is plain weave woven at the beginning and at the end of the inlaid pictorial tapestry. The heading is woven at about 2" wide by the entire length of the horizontal space of the tapestry's base.

This heading when doubled and threaded at the back of the tapestry's base provides an opening where a dowel or rod can be entered as a means of hanging the tapestry on the wall. This plain weave would also provide a structure of strength, since no thread ever passes over more than one other thread at a time in either of the shuttle's directions. This means that in a plain weaving, every weft thread passes over one warp thread and under one warp thread.

After you inlay wool on the first row, the previous sequences for both warp thread and weft thread are now opposite: under one and over the other. With gentle beating, each row of in-laid wool, the process is ready to be repeated in the next sequence of inlaid wool.

For both top and bottom headings (total of 4" x the width), there is not that great of warp count that you cannot learn by keeping records. To simplify the weft thread requirement, all you need to record is the total length of the headings.

The weft yarn needed for the total in-laid wool space of the tapestry, is divided it by ½" row of wool space per each weft. On our tapestry example 36" length will be as such:

36" length – 4" heading = 32" of total tapestry length for inlaid wool
32" divided by ½" = 72 rows of inlaid wool space.

With experience, you will be able to estimate the yarn requirements with enough accuracy for your next project.

WINDING THE WARP

A warping device has two purposes, a) it helps to hold the threads taut, so that each warp thread is exactly the same length b) it allows the establishment of the **cross,** the point at which the threads intersect from opposite directions in order to maintain their proper sequence. The role of the **cross** or **lease,** therefore is to keep the warp end in orderly position until the warp is threaded through the loom.

The most common warping pieces of equipment are the **reel** and the **warp-board.** The reel is much more expensive, but it permits a measure greater than 12 yards, and it is most commonly used to prepare the warp for floor or table loom. The warping board is a rectangular frame with removable pegs protruding from it. These pegs are set in a specific distance apart, often 1 yard. These wooden pegs are set to accommodate the desired distance to arrive at exact warp length.

You begin the procedure of winding warp by wrapping a guide string on the reel. This guide string, affixed on the reel frame establishes a path for the warp thread to follow as it is wound on the reel (or frame-board), so the correct length can be confirmed. The selected length of guiding string must be of another colour, and must represent the length of the warping frame of the floor loom.

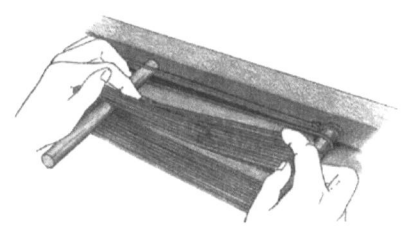

Start by selecting a guide string made from a strong cord in a colour that contrasts with the intended warp thread.

a) Cut the guide string 6" longer than the intended warp-length to allow for knotting at both ends of the reel.
b) Secure the guide string to the top of the reel.
c) As you rotate the reel, carry the guide string down diagonally to the bottom battery of wooden pegs.
d) If the guide string is too long or too short to be tied around the last peg at the bottom, adjust the angle of the diagonal descent until it fits exactly.
e) Make sure you pass the guide string **under** the first peg and over the second, and then tie to the third peg. (Follow the visual guide of the drawing)
f) The thread can now be warped following the visual path of the guide string.
g) Start the warp at the bottom of the reel by tying the thread to the first peg at the horizontal bar.

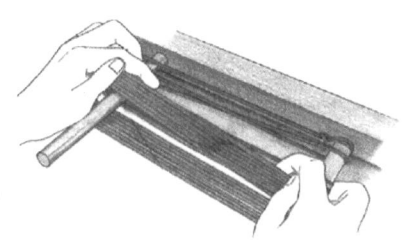

h) There is also a horizontal bar at the top of the reel around whose pegs the cross or lease is formed.

i) Only one cross or lease is necessary, but two are recommended for the beginner in case one of the crosses is lost.

j) Do not warp the threads on top of each other. Instead lay them as close as possible on the pegs. This way you can maintain an even tension throughout the winding process, so that all warps are exactly the same length.

k) To make the intended warp with crosses at both top and bottom horizontal bars (follow the drawing), tie the beginning in place around the peg 'A'.

l) Go under peg 'B' and upwards around as often as necessary for the desired length.

m) Now go under peg "C' and over peg 'D' and 'E'. Continue by returning under peg 'E' and 'D', and over peg 'C', return descending around to 'B', then over 'B' and back under 'A'.

n) Continue by repeating this process until the total number of warps ends is completed. If the end is at an even number, tie and cut off at peg 'A', if it is an odd number tie and cut off at peg 'E'.

As stated previously, it is advisable to make a second lease either on top or the bottom of the horizontal bars. If you are a beginner in the process of warping, this double lease will keep the threads from being lost or tangled.

WALK YOUR FINGERS AND CHAIN

In order to easily remove and carry away the warp from the reel or warping board, you must count groups of threads and chain the warp in order to reduce its length.

'Walk your fingers' means to count the yarns on the reel. The best and fastest way to count is to use your fingers and separate each thread, by pulling one at a time towards you.

When you separate the first group of even or odd number of threads, tie a heavy yarn around each group.

For example, if the total number of yarns is 120, you may wish to form a group of 6 of 20 yarns each. Use as many ties as necessary through the entire length of the warp in order to stabilize it.

If you seem to find it difficult keeping count of threads, mark off every group of 20 (as your warping) and tie with a contrasting yarn. When you finish warping, you may wish to make a number of choke ties to prevent the warp from tangling when removed and transferred to the loom. Remember to always tie the cross itself as well at either side of the cross and within 6". Begin to chain the yarn starting at the bottom first peg. Put your right hand through the first loop and pull the yarn through to form the next loop. Continue the process until you reach the top and slip the last chained loop into position.

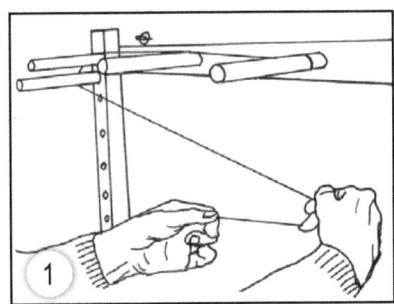
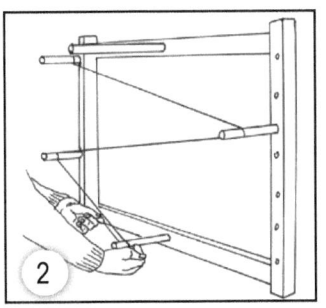
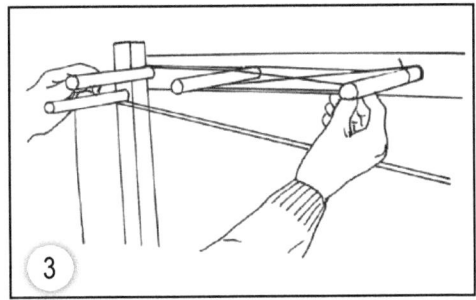

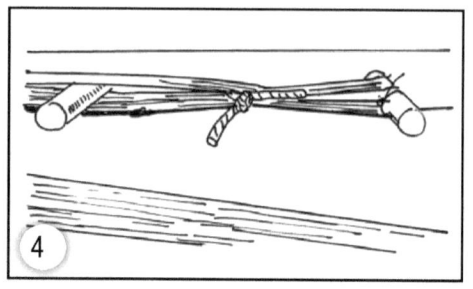

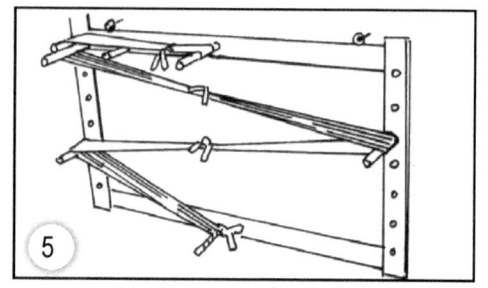

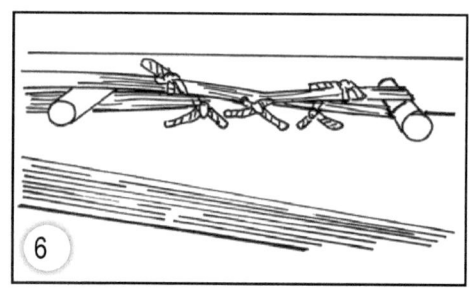

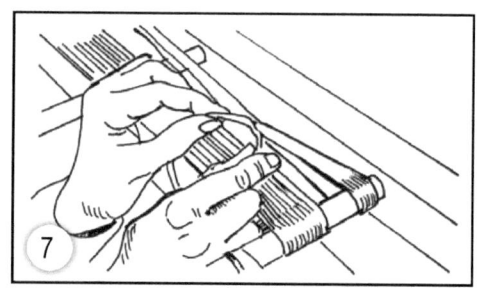

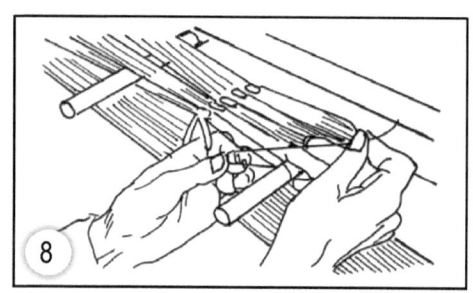

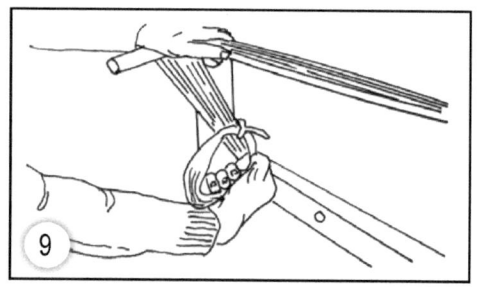

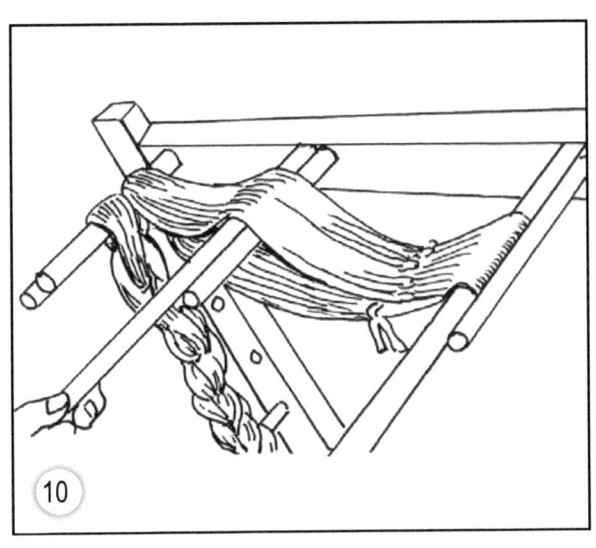

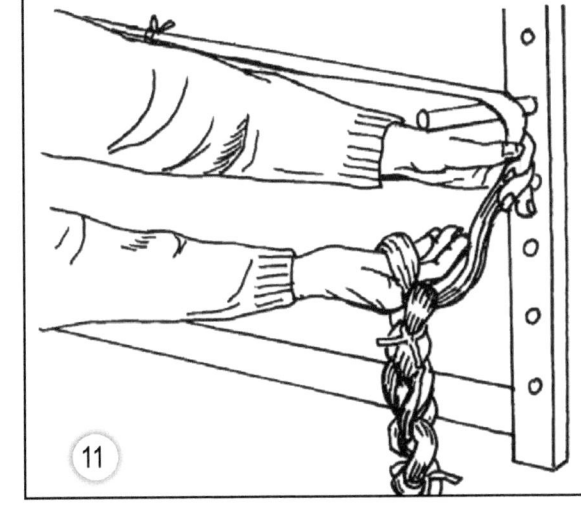

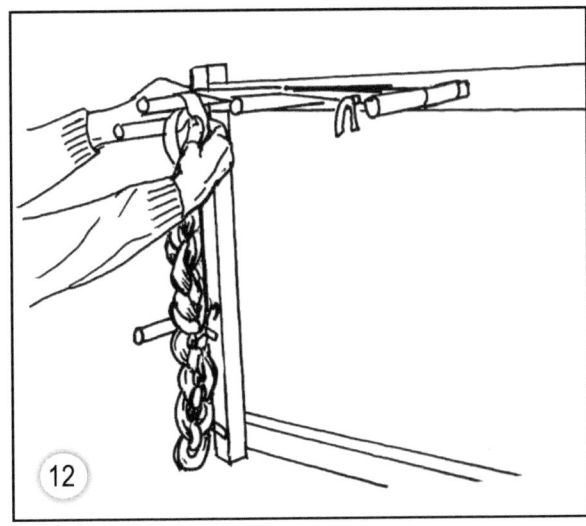

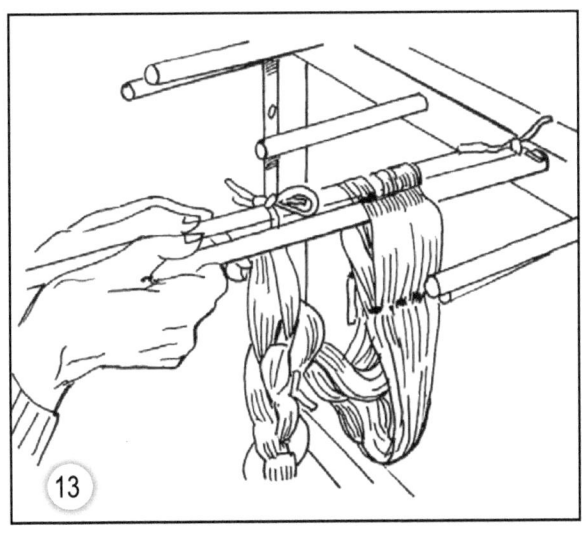

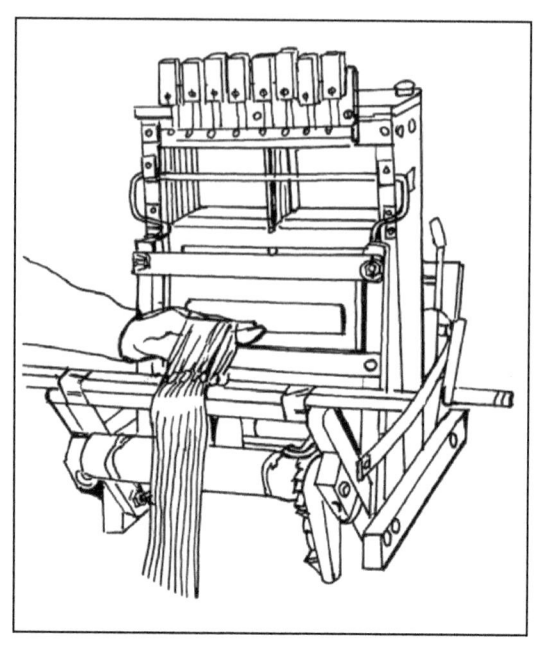
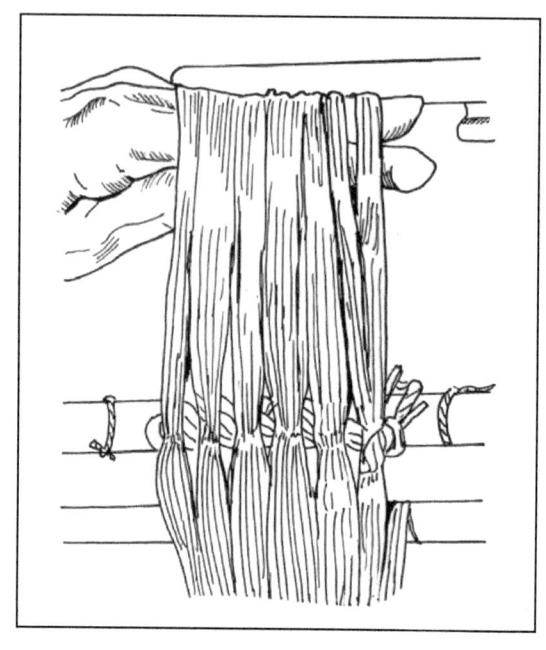

REMOVING THE CHAINED WARP AND DRESSING THE LOOM

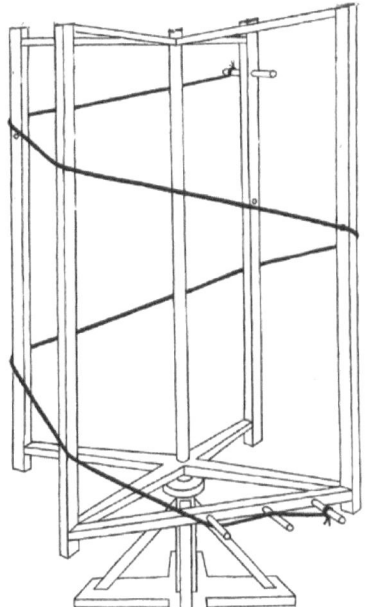

After the chained warp has been removed from the reel and taken to the loom, it must be rolled onto the warp beam, then drawn-in through the heddles, threaded through the beater reed, and attached onto the fabric beam. One way of warping is the back to front method. The other way is front to back. Which warping method you use depends on individual choice: there is no "right" or "wrong" method.

For our purpose, we will roll the warp onto the warp beam and thread from the back of the loom to the front. First thing you must do is to check that you have enough **inserted eye** metal heddles on each of the two harnesses. Using our current example of 120 warp threads, you must count 120 heddles. You must remove any extra heddles by tying them back to the side of the shaft and out of the way. Check once again that the metal heddles are all asymmetrical. The bottom and top twist should not be in opposite direction; they are set correctly when all "eyes slant" in the same direction. This way, when the yarn is inserted it would lie in a straight line. Next, we know that our warp example is tied in groups of 20 yarns, so you may wish to bundle up the heddles in a group of 10 (6 groups for each harness). We begin with:

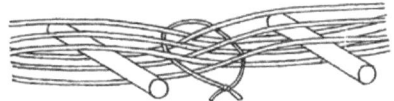

a) Attach the chained warp to the metal rod by the back beam. This is done by inserting the metal rod in the looped end of the warp. Secure the metal rod temporarily onto the back beam.

b) Spread all 6 groups of 20 yarns evenly to the width that is to be woven. Insert the **lease sticks** into the warp on either side of the cross and tie them as close to the centre of the cross as possible. The lease sticks will maintain the cross while the warp is being threaded and beamed, and are removed when the process of sleying is finished.

c) Unchain all 6 groups of yarns with sufficient length to reach over the castle, and attach weights to maintain temporary tension.

d) Start with the first group of 20 yarns and thread **alternately** on harness "A" and harness "B", so that 10 alternate threaded heddles on harness "A", and 10 threaded heddles on harness "B" will complete 20 heddles (see related drawing.) Tie each bundle of 20 yarns behind the heddles with a slipknot to prevent entanglement.

e) Continue threading the heddles until all 6 groups of 20 yarns have alternately passed through harness "A" and "B".

f) When the threading is done, you should have the same number of the threads with heddles. Check for threading errors. This is the time to correct them.

ROLL ON THE WARP

This is the last step in the loom dressing: tying up the warp to the fabric beam at the front of the loom.
The process is as follows:

- Bring the fabric stick, which is attached to the fabric beam, over the breast beam.
- Take the 10th group from the beater reed and pull the yarns towards the breast beam and over and around the cloth stick.
- Divide this group of 20 yarns in proper sequence. Carry each group of 10 yarns around the cloth stick and tie them in a half-knot.
- Repeat this process first with group yarn number 20 (extreme left) and then with group number 1 to extreme right.
- Continue alternating groups of yarn to the left and to the right, until all 20 groups of warp are tied to the fabric stick.

- It is most important to have equal tension across the warp. If you are a beginner, now is the time to ask an experienced friend to help with the final stages of dressing the loom.
- Make any adjustments necessary and check for threading errors. Some of the common errors are a) missed yarn, b) missed heddles, c) crossed threads, d) a missed dent.
- When the final inspection is done, and all errors corrected, complete all ties with a bowknot.

It is now time to wind the warp on the warp beam by turning the crank.

- Remove the back rod and tie onto the warp beam.
- From the front (have a friend), untie the fabric rod and carry it with the tied yarns as far back as permitted. Keep even tension. Strum the warp with the back of your hand (like a guitar) to get rid of tangling.
- Turn the crank on the warp beam and make sure you turn it the correct direction. As the warp beam is rolled around insert a corrugated paper between the warp and warp beam, and about the width of the project.
- Do not use newspaper or other material that may leave grease residue.
- As you crank and roll the warp beam, your friend at the front end must maintain an even tension while approaching near the fabric beam.
- When your helper reaches the fabric beam put on the break on the warp beam. You can now go to the front and secure the fabric stick onto the fabric beam.
- Check that the yarns are in the same direction with the beater reed, that they are spaced evenly, and that they have equal tension

BEATER REED

A beater reed is an essential part of the loom, for it spaces the warp ends in according to the plan, and by back and forth movement, it beats the laid in wool in place.

Reeds are available with 6,8,10,12 dents per inch, though you may also find other sizes. Most reeds tend to rust in humid climates. It is advisable to make a good investment by purchasing stainless steel reeds.

When choosing reeds, you may wish to consider what **setts** you will normally use and what reeds are most versatile.

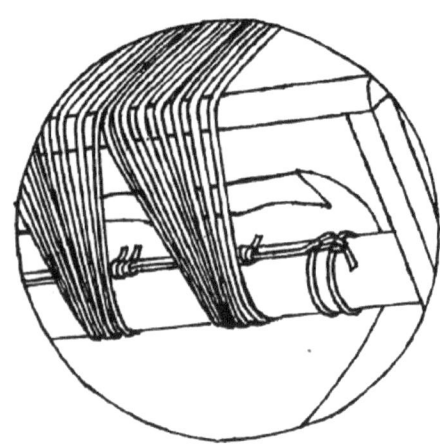

If you plan to use the reed for other projects, aside from laid in wool which requires 6 or 8 dents per inch, you may wish to consider the following: a 20 dent per inch reed will also give you a 6,8, or 10 dent per inch by simply skipping other dents. As with heddles, the direction of sleying the beater reed is a question of personal preference left to right, right to left. Left-handed weavers often find it much more easy to begin at the left hand end.

- Untie the first group of 20 yarns from the heddle frame "A" and "B"
- Take each yarn in precisely the same sequence and direction as they occur in the heddles to avoid errors.
- Draw in the yarns through the dents with a sley hook or reed hook.
- After each group of 20 yarns is sleyed, tie it behind the reed with a slipknot to prevent the threads from falling out of the reed. Continue with the process.
- Measure from the extreme left edge of the warp on the reed to the extreme edge to the right. The measurement should correspond with the width of the intended woven project.

TIE UP THE HARNESSES

Threddles are connected by **lamms** to the harnesses. The connections are varied to serve the needs of a particular weaving pattern. As such, the threadles must be tied to the lamms for each individual harness separately. This way "A" threadle raises harness "A" and threadle "B" raises harness "B". This is a standard tie up, which function includes the plain weaving.

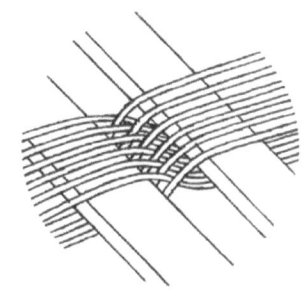

Harness "A" and "B" must be positioned to serve the left and right foot accordingly. The method of connecting the lamms to the harnesses and the threadles to the lamms depends upon how the floor loom is designed. Some floor looms are equipped with metal connectors, others have cords with snap locks, and still others provided none of the above, the cords must be tied individually.

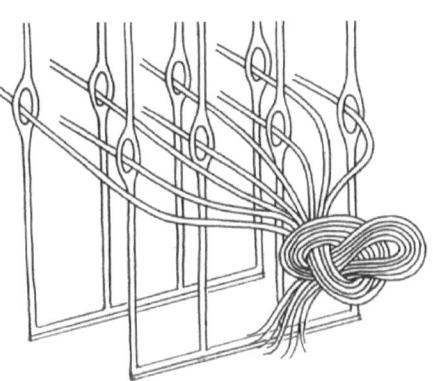

In a 2-harness floor loom, the harnesses remain in the raised position when the threadle is depressed. When the foot (right or left) is removed from the threadle, the harness drop and shed is shut. With this simple threading sequence that alternates the left and right foot it provides a steady and most efficient rhythm.

PLAIN WEAVE, IN-LAID WOOL & 2 HARNESS LOOM

Of the floor loom weaves, the most basic is the plain weave. We are all surrounded by such a weave in our daily lives from handkerchiefs to bed linens.

Plain weave is simple. The first weft shot goes over one warp yarn and under one and repeats across the width of the tapestry. In the second row, the weft alternates and goes over the warp yarn it had already gone under. The third row repeats the first, the fourth row repeats the second, and so on. As you notice, this weave is a repetitive process of two weft shots.

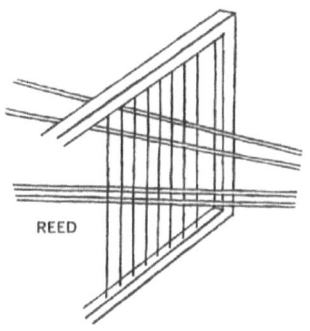

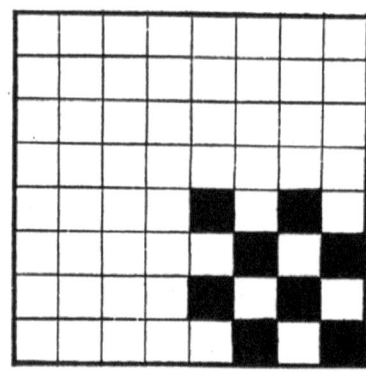

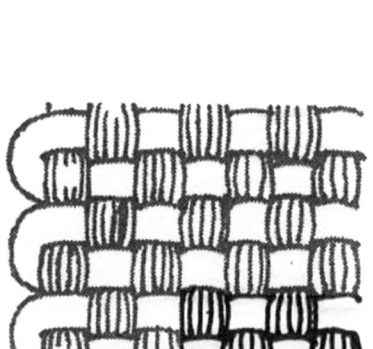

This is possible as long as all even number warp yarns (2,4,6,8...) are always raised on one shed (harness "A"), and all odd number warp yarns (1,3,5,7...) are raised on the other shed (harness "B").

Therefore, only the plain weave can be done so easily on the 2-harness floor loom, since there are just two shed possibilities.

In the heading of the in-laid tapestry you continue with the plain weave until you have completed 2 inches of fabric. As the in-laid wool progresses you simply interlock the wool with weft shots. When you have completed the required 2 inches of heading, stitch the beginning of the fabric using the **blanket** or **overcast** method. You may wish to stitch with the same colour of thread.

This whole process must be completed before you roll the tapestry on the fabric beam.

When the whole in-laid wool tapestry is finished, plain weave the final heading; stitch the end; fold the heading back on itself, and stitch it before cutting off the warp ends.

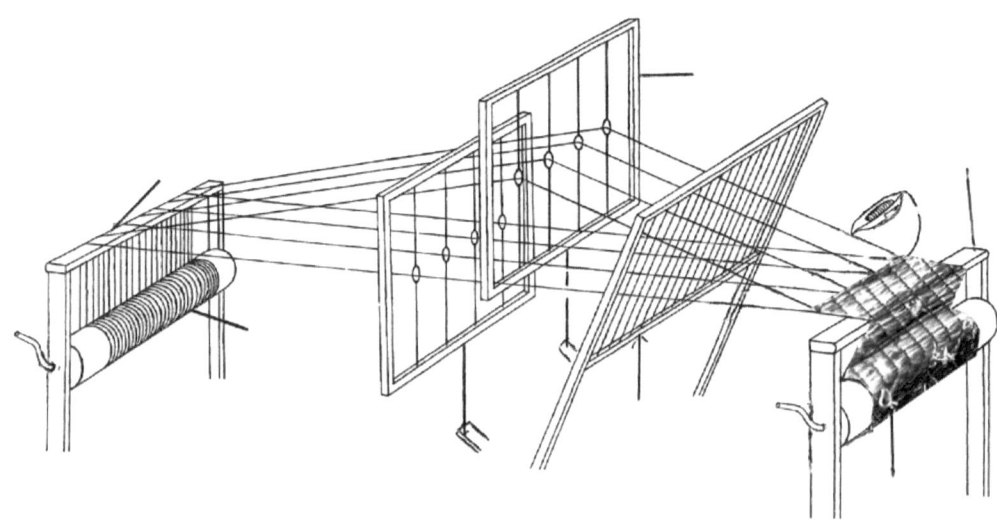

PROFILE DRAFTING: THE CARTOON

The tapestry cartoon is the preliminary profile drafting used as a guide by the inlaid tapessier. Most of the great masters have prepared their theme for tapestry (their profile draftings still survive today), and some are shown as oil paintings. Today, the more usual medium is watercolour. Depending on the intricacy of the design, most often the cartoon is drawn to scale for enlargement on the loom. Major outlines and block pattern areas can be transferred directly to the warp yarns by marking them with felt tipped pens. **Block pattern** areas are the squares in the grid system, some made from wire, nylon, or scrapped on paper. Choose the kind of ink that will not rub off during the handling process.

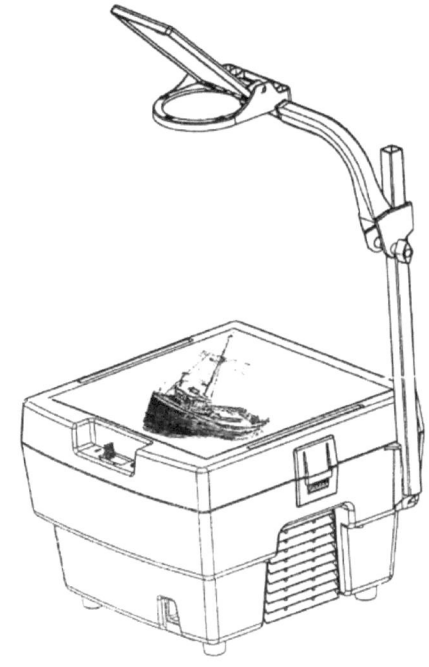

Because of the medium, a tapessier of in-laid is often depicting indoor scenes or outdoor landscape imagery. You may use photographic blow-ups, overheads, and slide projectors as the means of transferring the imagery into a grid system.

STARTING AT THE BEGINNING

In the early attempts at drafting, it can be difficult to decide just how much of what we can see in front of us should be put down on the drafting paper. We usually focus on the scene in front of our vision. There is almost a sense in which we can see peripherally around us. However, if we consider how much we can focus on, within the limitations of a conventional perspective approach, we soon realize that is extremely difficult to get the entire landscape into an in-laid tapestry theme. Therefore, we need to be selective, narrow in the angle of vision so that our theme may focus on only a fraction of what we see in the natural landscape.

When selecting your subject, focus on the part of the landscape and make a drawing of the object you can comfortably take in within a relative narrow angle of vision. You can attempt to draw a much wider view.

In the photograph to the upper right, you can notice that the trees are curving in towards your vision, (that is, to the left and right at the periphery of your vision, and of the ground close to your feet). You can notice that, a focus in the middle distance concentrates on a tree that is clearly defined. This is how a conventional line of perspective works because the objects, subjects, or scenes are generally contained within a 60-degree angle of vision (bottom right).

In a wider-angle view, the drawing encompasses an extremely wide angle of vision. In this sense, it demonstrates that a drawing taking in such a wide angle of view can generate a real sense of involvement and of place. Focusing on a selective angle vision, on the other hand, within the larger landscaping, works best before the image begins to distort as the limits of the core vision is arched. The choice is yours.

NATURAL PERSPECTIVE: SKETCHING GLASS

When you draw a landscape in perspective, the object seen through a sheet of glass (8"x10" or 20cm x 25cm) passes ight rays from the object to your eyes. That is, the objects that are drawn on your sheet of paper are shown as they would be seen when viewed through a transparent surface. When you make a drawing on a sheet of glass of the view seen through it, you will see for yourself some of the aforementioned basic principles of linear perspective drawing.

If you are a beginner, start drawing small objects i.e., a small pot of flowers, a bottle, a book, or a vase sitting on top of your kitchen table.

1) Try to keep the glass frame in a fixed position, or else, the image will wobble around. Keep your head in the same position. Use one eye only when you draw.

2) By moving your object forwards or backwards, you can alter the size of your image. Moving the object towards you, the image of the subject will appear larger on the glass.

3) To transfer the image, place a damp sheet of paper on the glass. This way, you can transfer a reverse image of what you have drawn.

4) When you peel the paper off, the image will have been transferred on the paper. A more convenient method is to place the image on top of a light box. Put your paper on top of the glass and redraw the image. You may want to re-size the composition by using a photocopier.

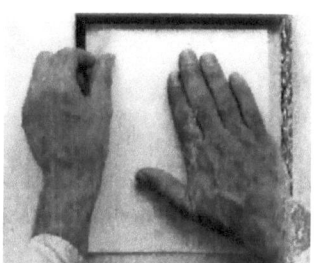

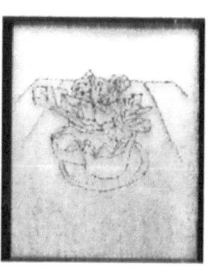
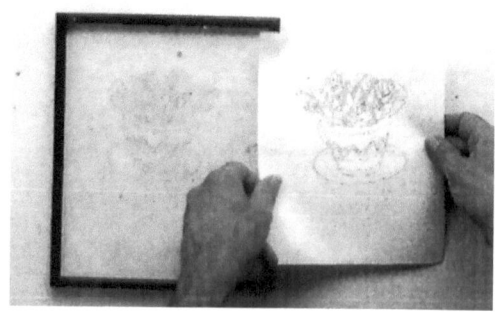

THE USE OF PHOTOGRAPHIC CAMERAS AND SLIDE PROJECTORS.

Fibre artists who are attracted to indoor scenes or outdoor landscapes often take photographic slides of interesting subjects that they want to transfer onto an inlaid tapestry, and also for future reference.

However, a standard lens in a popular camera would not do the job. Common cameras are instruments that take a relative wide-angle picture, and do not allow you to zoom in as your eye would. For our purpose, use a camera with a lens of variable focal length, from 28mm (wide angle) to 260mm (telephoto). This aperture allows you to focus on whichever section of the landscape you wish to include.

You might make photographic slides in order to draw an image by using a projector. When using a projector you must have enough ambient light to allow you to see what your drawing pencil on the sketch paper is doing on the wall. Reversely, if you have too much ambient light you cannot see the projected image or the lines. Make sure that your slide projector is on a 90-degree level and is focused squarely on the paper to avoid any distortion of the image.

In order to enlarge or reduce your image by this method you need a slide projector with a lens of variable focal length. This way you can make the image bigger or smaller by rotating the lens to and from the sketch paper.

Using a slide projector with a variable focal length, you can crop the image and establish the composition that suits your ideas for your tapestry. This way you capture the essential components.

Finally, draw enough details to allow you to develop the cartoon in the way you want. You must also remember that since your slide projector gets hot, and the slides remain in it for some time, the slide projector must have an internal electric fan to keep it cool.

With the right kind of overhead projector, it is quite possible to enlarge the image to the desired size of the tapestry you are planning to create. This makes it easier to transfer the cartoon onto the warp yarn.

REPRODUCING A PICTURE

GRID SYSTEM: Take a photograph or original artwork and enlarge it on a copy machine. This is a quick method of 'duplication' of a picture if you need to alter the size of duplication. To do thusly, you have to decide the exact size of your tapestry – width and length. You will use a ruler to draw a grid. By doing this, you are now able to see a group of shapes. You have broken the picture down into puzzle pieces, simplifying it and making it much easier to draw.

Practice this yourself. Lightly draw a grid on your drawing paper with a pencil and ruler. To make your drawing the same size as the photo, make your puzzle pieces the same size. To make your drawing smaller, make the squares smaller on your paper. As long as the squares are identical to each other, it does not matter. You can also use the same method to enlarge by making the squares on your paper larger than the ones on the picture (photocopy).

To acheieve the line of the subject you draw what you see, from one square to another. Soon you'll see wherer each shape lines up within each square. Always watch for accuracy. Draw lightly, as these lines must be erased as needed when your sketch is completed. Once you are sure that your drawing is accurate in its shape, you can begin by adding detail and tones.

TRANSFER CARTOON ONTO WARP YARN:

The inlaid tapestry cartoon is the preliminary drawing used as a guide by the weaver. Major outlines and pattern areas can be transferred dicectly to the warp yarns by marking them with a neutral colour felt tipped pen. The ink should not rub off during the in-laid process, and the inlaid wool in the finished tapestry will obscure it.

To transfer the full size cartoon square blocks directly onto the warp yarns and cut off a horizontal set of squares from your paper. Insert this set of squares in the middle of the warp threads with the image facing upwards. Looking downwards transfer the outlines of each square onto the warp yarns.

GRID SYSTEM:

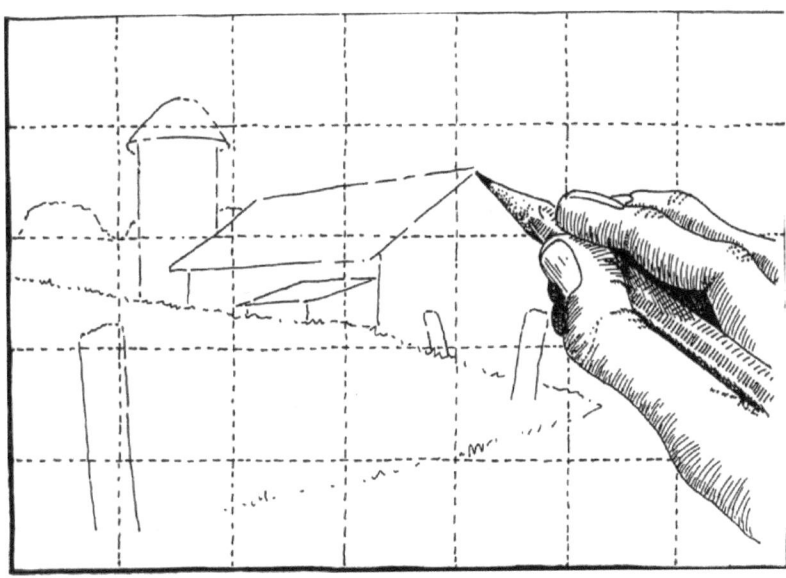

Finish each of the horizontal sections, and insert the next set of horizontal cartoon squares between the warp yarns. Repeat the process of transferring the cartoon onto the warp yarns.

DIRECT TRANSFER:

Chapter 5
FROM LOOSE WOOL TO DYED ROLAG

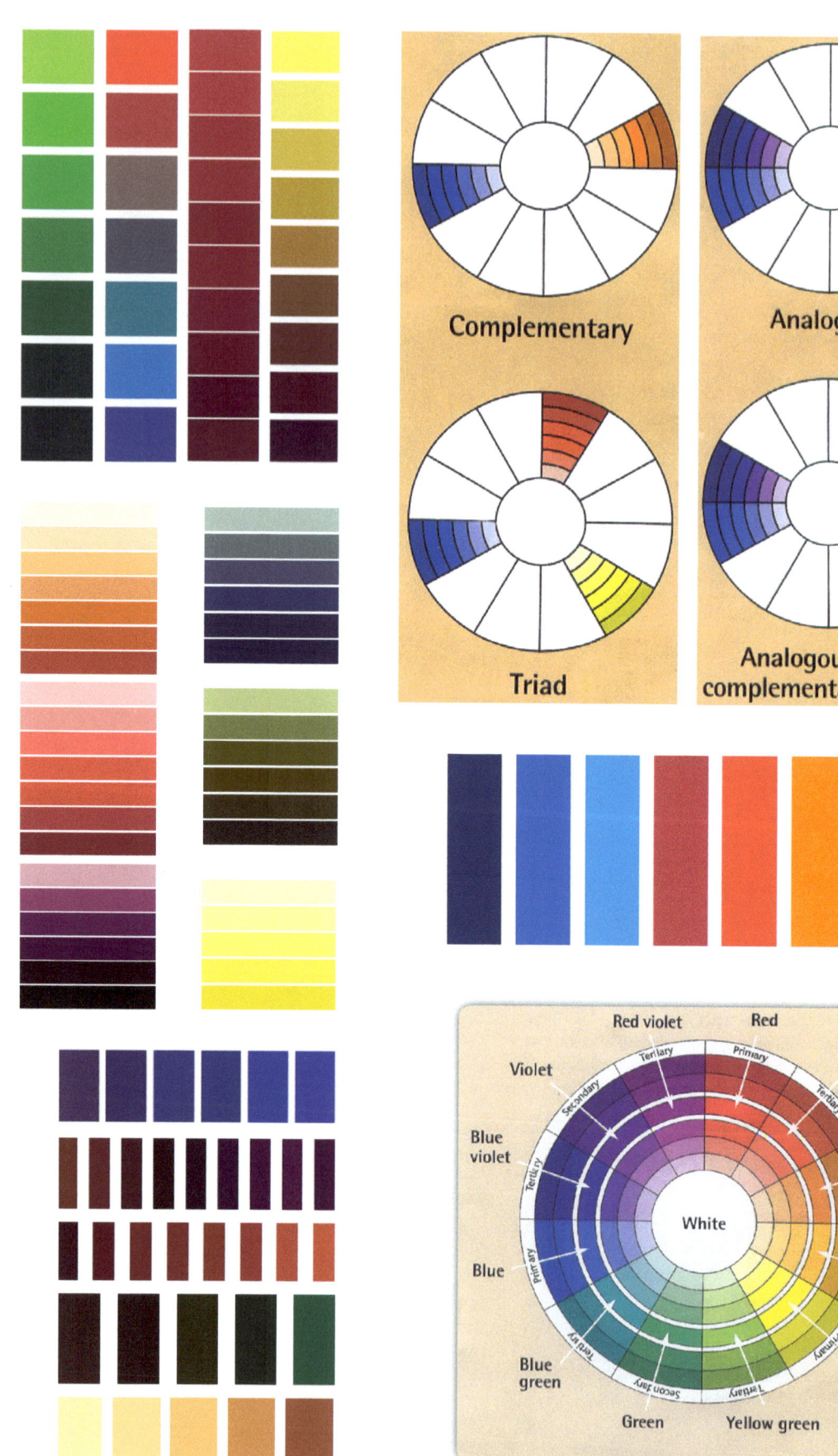

MACHINE CARDING WOOL

Since dyed wool is the primary material used in in-laid tapestry, it is necessary to stock a sufficient amount and variety of shades, tones and colours. While finger-carding can provide you with small quantities of colour wool, it would be wise to invest in a mechanized wool carder to meet your needs for both colour variety and amount. Mechanized carders come in different sizes. Choose one that would meet the need of your projects.

Picture 2, show the carders' foot control pedal over the dram's speed. Speed is increased as the wool is transferred from the carder's hand onto the drum.

Using a wirebrush, the carder removes wool as carefully as possible while turning the drum by hand. This flat mass of carded wool will be separated into 3 or 4 streamed sections to be made into rolag.

It should be noted that, when there is a need for mixing colour backgrounds of wools, now is the time to do the mixing. Two or more colours, or shades of tones, can be carded together at once to achieve desired background shade results.

MAKING A ROLAG

As previously mentioned, mechanized carded wool is flat in form when removed from the drum. This flat shape presents an inconvenience in terms of space and material control. The artist needs small quantities of wool every time he/she inlays. Therefore, there is a necessity to separate portions of flat-shaped wool into a manageable amount. A rolag is the final stage of wool readiness.

You may wish to divide the wool into 2 – 3 sections. Role it loosely over your knee while simultaneously pulling it away from its center. Do this until you have a certain length (about 3 feet) forming a loose rolag (see pictures 7, 8 and 9).

As viewed in pictures 11 and 12, there are some necessary tools needed to produce large amounts of rolags. This is only when you are planning several projects ahead, with a large requirement of rolag: needing a variety of colours, shades and tones.

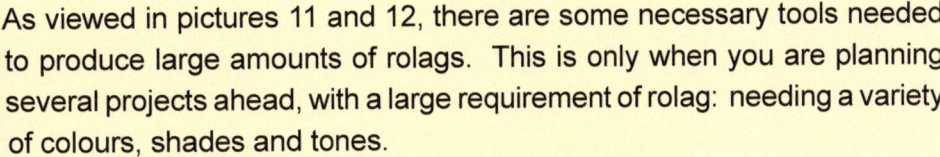

A kitchen table of proportional length and a cloth is necessary to provide a sturdy space to roll. A wooden board with an appropriate handle is a must. When moved back and forth, over the loose rolag, it would tighten the wool into manageable tubular shape.

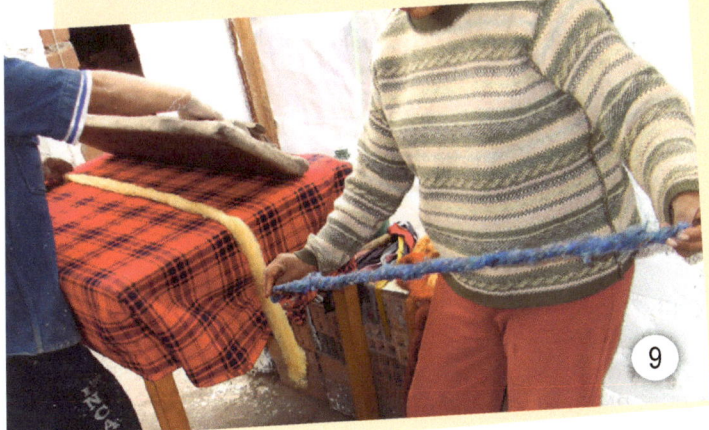

As you can see, this hand-held wooden board is dressed with a canvass and it is held with both hands. A harmonious movement or rolling it back and forth, with an appropriate downward pressure, will ensure an evenly sized rolag.

The results are evident. Rolags of multitude colour, shades and tones are ready to be used. Of those multitude colours, the tapessier would combine two or more to create a method of finger-carding: a unique mixture of colour background as needed.

Having available a multitude of single colour rolags placed over the beater bar can be a problem of space. The tapessier must have these rolags in front of him/her for work-convenience, and rolling them as tight as possible can provide an extra space.

In the chapter entitled Dyer's Studio, there are numerous recipes for both natural and artificial dyeing processes. A large number of primary, secondary, tertiary and complementary colours, tones and shades can be created from among the afore-mentioned classifications of colours.

Yet, it seems, there is always a colour, tone or shade that appears to be missing from our ready made stock. With a little practice, however, you can utilize colours that are available to you to create different tones and shades of the same colour, thus, providing you with different options of shades. A deep olive green can be modified at the point where you are mixing two different shades of green to make a medium or light shade. Finger-carding provides a perfect mix of two or more colours to achieve the tone or shade desired.

This is an identical process of colour mixing, or shade mixing, as is available to a painter who is about to mix two or three different tones to create a desired shade of his/her choice. In our case, a fibre artist mixes different tones of dyed wool instead of paint.

As such, the process of mixing colours, tones and shades is a constant factor in creating outstanding tones and shades for every step in the process of in-laying wool. More about this is presented to you in pictures in the in-laying weaving section of the book.

This (picture 12) represents a standard method of set-up at every beginning of a Pictorial Tapestry in the making: a cartoon picture, a number of rolags and the plain weave support (attached onto the front bar).

Chapter 6
BASIC TOOLS AND THEIR FUNCTION

THE USE OF METAL PICKER

USING THE METAL PICKER:

The metal picker is a simple tool that everyone can make by simply purchasing a thin screwdriver and using it as required. With it you can do the following:

(a) Spread widely wool you just in-laid.
(b) You can add on top of a background different colour, shade or tone of wool and direct it to a specific position.
(c) By poking, pulling and pushing in-laid wool you can form general background, specific distinctive-lines, direct a dark or light shade into its respective position, i.e., between two or more distinctive colours, shades and tones.
(d) You can do corrections (even after the scale is completed) by inserting a mixed amount of wool between the warp threads. For example, if a background has a strong colour (red) and you need to tone it down, you may add a bit of orange on top of the red to give it a

more harmonious appearance. Blue sky that appears too blue can be reduced by adding bits of white to tone it down as well. The same applies for sea, forest, house colours, etc.

A scale is a horizontal tapestry space between a set of two weft threads. It is approximately a 1/2" width times the length of the tapestry (selvedge to selvedge).

Within the scale, the fibre artist in-lays small amounts of finger-carded wool and in-lays it between the upper and lower level of the warp. The metal picker is, therefore, used to direct, wide spread or concentrate such wool to its proper position.

No in-laying of wool can take place without the use of the metal picker. It is used every time you in-lay wool into a scale. Taken from the rolag, a single or mixed colour of wool is finger-carded and in-laid in the tapestry's scale. Picture 13 shows two finger-mixed

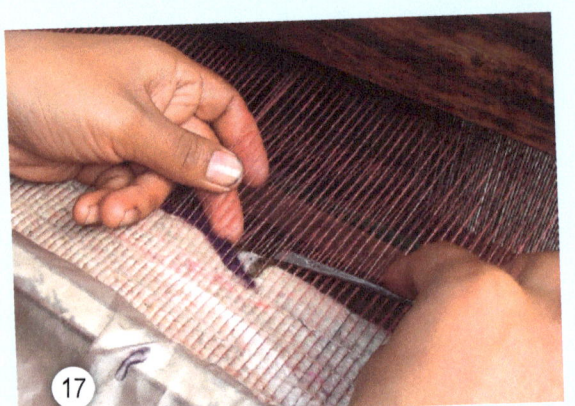

colours of wool about to be in-laid. With the help of the metal picker, it would be smoothed and spread horizontally within the tapestry's scale. Picture 16 shows a single colour wool in-laid between warp threads.

A multi-purpose tool, the metal picker, is the size of a small screwdriver of about 8" long (without the handle). It is flat on one end in order to slide easily between the warp threads and the in-laid wool. In order to avoid accidentally cutting the warp threads, the flat-end would be dull.

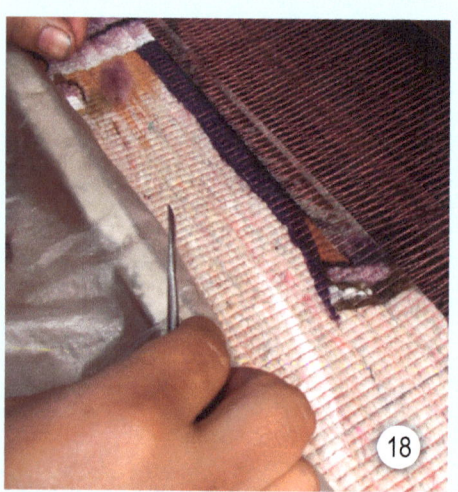

By stroking counter-clockwise over the in-laid wool, the metal picker ensures that the wool is under the warp threads and in its correct position.

By poking, pulling and spreading, the metal picker can remove extra wool that is more than the necessary amount needed. For example, in pictures 18 and 19, a lightly spread blue

wool over a deep colour brownish background gives the effect of a morning mist. In this case, the metal picker is used to 'widespread' the blue wool (allowing it to show through the deep colour background).

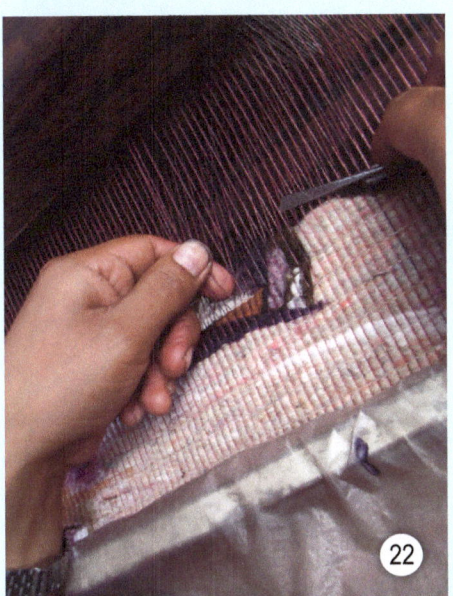

Picture 22, shows the metal picker positioning in-laid wool; picture 18 depicts a small amount directed to a more intricate position. Pictures 19 to 21 have the metal picker used in a multi-complex in-laid wool design; as I have said, the picker is an indispensable tool.

In pictures 21, 22 and 23, the metal picker is used to direct and form a distinctive-sharp-separation between two or more colour of wool. In pictures 22 and 23, the metal picker is used to form a distinctive-sharp-line between two or more colours.

GENERAL OBSERVATIONS

MULTIPLE SHADE BACKGROUND:

A forest with different shades and tones of lighter or darker green wool can be achieved by mixing and carding. Just pull the wool and mix and by adding more of your desired shade until you are satisfied with the results. Then in-

lay these mixtures at the appropriate position. Should you require brown or yellow or orange colour (at certain points within the overall green background), just add on top of the previously in-laid amount and spread the colours with the help of the metal picker. You can spread those mixed purposefully unevenly to give a distinctive character of a fall appearance of the forest.

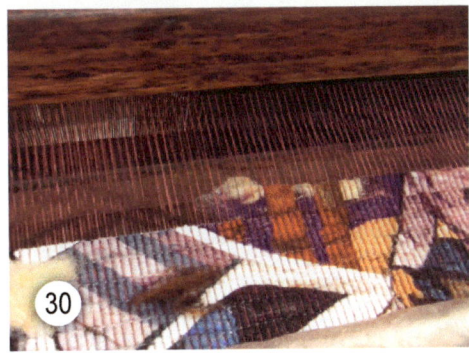

CREATING A MORNING MIST:

This effect requires a darker background of in-laid wool of a variety of shades representing a forest, or country road, a mist over water, etc. Over such background you must in-lay the whitest wool this is available to you (whether natural or artificial) that would 'show' the background through it. Placing a thin layer of white wool over the darker background and spread with the metal picker and provided 'openings' where the darker background would 'show' is the correct way to do it. The same applies to creating a morning mist over a 'structural' object such as a roof of a building, a night street, over a night-time line (nocturnal) or over a country fence. The amount of forefront white wool you intend to place over the background would determine the quality of representational aspect of the overall theme you intend to create. So, use the metal picker to spread the over-laid wool and guide into its proper place.

REMOVING A SCALE OF IN-LAID WOOL:

At times, for both a novice and an experienced tapessier, it is necessary to remove rather than correct a scale which (for obvious reasons) didn't come out to its correct creation. The removal of a scale is easily done. Simply remove the weft yarns backwards and remove the in-laid wool to your desired level (or all of it, or various scales previously in-laid). It is better to start all over again **than continue toward back results of a scale that would 'stick' out-as-a-sore-thumb. Remember, removing a scale is not a waste of time; it is an attempt on your part to create something better than you had before.**

TEMPLE STICK

Warp in-take. As a normal procedure the weft is woven 3 times for every scale. As weft-thread is woven and beaten into place, the warp rolls over and under each scale's weft. Warp weave tension, therefore, affects the amount of in-take in the overall length of the tapestry itself.

The narrower the scale is, the more the warp interlaces with the weft, and the greater the in-take (or shrinkage) of the tapestry. Because the in-take shortens the warp, you must plan this into each project. It is advisable to in-lay 5 to 10 scales extra in the tapestry length warp-end, which, when in-take occurs place, would not be noticeable.

Weft in-take. The weft also has in-take because its 3 passes must travel over and under each warp. In addition, the weft catches the selvedge which tends to draw-in the edge. To prevent draw-in, you must use a template (shown in picture 31 and 32) which hooks at the end of each selvedge.

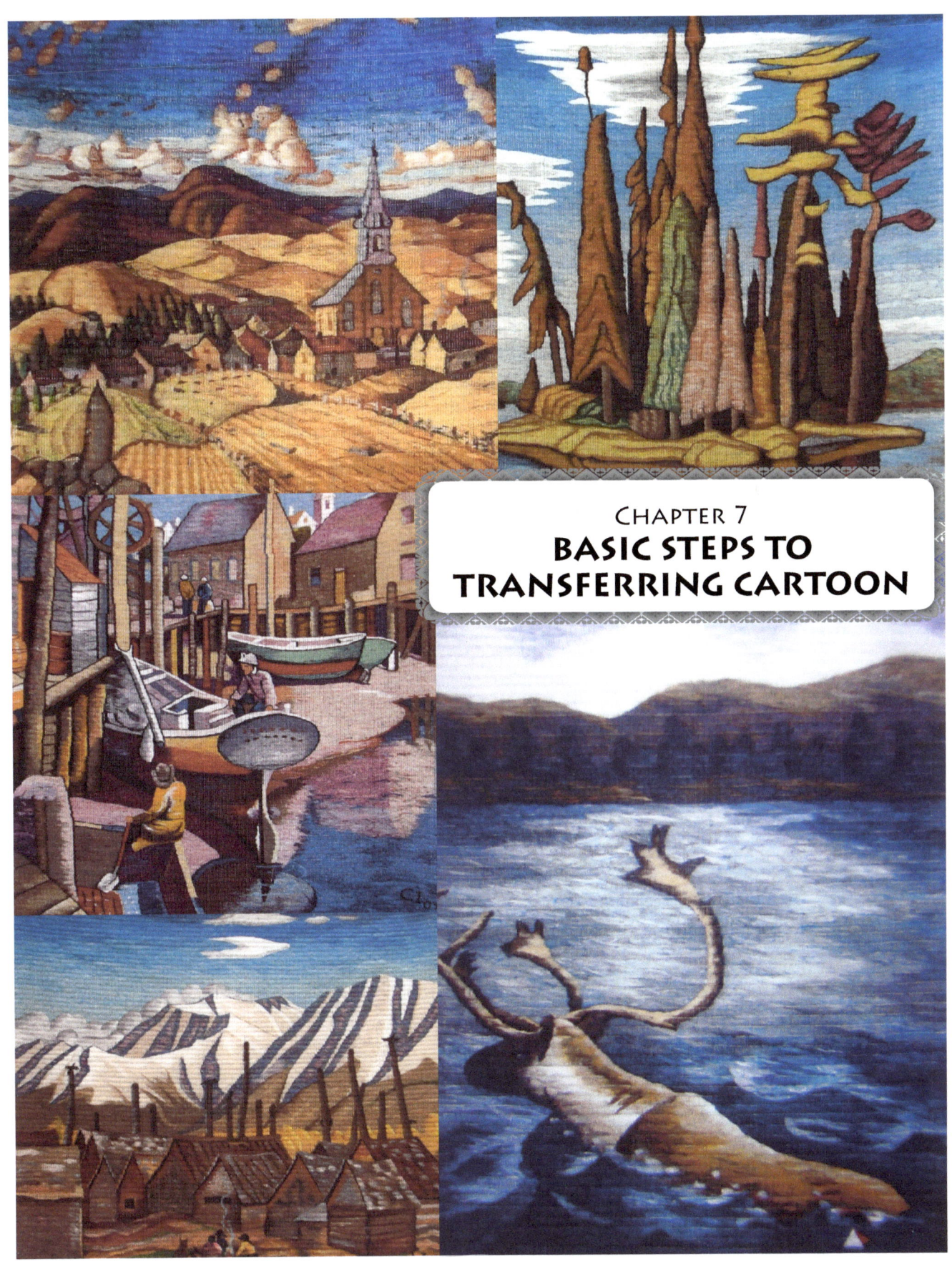

Chapter 7
BASIC STEPS TO TRANSFERRING CARTOON

BASIC STEPS TO TRANSFERRING CARTOON

TRANSFERRING DESIGN CARTOON ONTO THE WARP THREADS:

BASIC STEPS

All square blocks must be identical in size. This way the overall tapestry design is identically divided into equal parts in order for the fibre artist to follow an equilibrium of space.

The horizontal and vertical set of square blocks can be small or large in their measurement, so long as they are identical in size (see pictures 33 and 35 the number of vertical square blocks also maybe larger than the horizontal ones, versus the vertical ones; this would depend on the requirements of each design.

In picture 34, the fibre artist is using a steel pin dipped in dye (black) colour, and is marking the measurement of each of the square blocks (both vertical and horizontal) on warp yarn.

In picture 33, a proper place to position the picture with the grid is just above the heddles. This way the fibre artist has the overall design at close range.

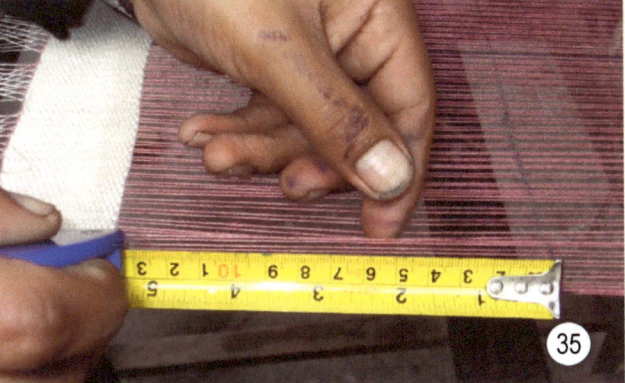

Pictures 33 and 35. Depending on the overall or specific sections of the tapestry's background colour or tone, it is necessary to dye those sections (or leave them un-dyed if required) so that the shade of warp lines will not show

on the surface of the tapestry (which could distort the colour or tone of the image that is weaved). Using a shoe brush dipped in a dye-tone of your choice, dye the warp threads. This is done after the plain weave (support) is in place.

In general it is recommended that the warp threads be of neutral colour. This way you could dye them according to the overall or partial background of the theme to be weaved. As you can see in picture 37, the entire warp yarns are dyed in one colour (red) to accommodate the requirements. On the other hand, in picture 36, the red dye has been placed partially onto the warp yarns leaving the rest of the space in neutral colour.

Picture 37. Depending on the size of your loom, you may draw one or two sets of square blocks at a time. Therefore the process of measuring dyed square blocks, as needed, and drawing the general outlines of the design itself is an on-going procedure. Here you can see a close-up of both square blocks and outlines

of the design itself. In picture 37, the weaving process has been advanced to the point where the fibre artist must draw further square blocks and continue with the outlines of the theme itself.

Picture 39, and 40. Following the transferring of the square blocks onto the warp yarn, the artist begins the general outline of the cartoon design.

Pictures 39. Another technique of dyeing warp yarn in small sections is to use a toothbrush. This way you could dye sections of warp yarns that follow a specific tapestry design with one or more colours as required. Those colours must be matched with the shade of the in-laid intended wool. Picture 36 shows different sections of varying colours while other sections remain neutral. Whereas dyeing the warp threads helps bring out the colours desired, at the same time, if dyed wool yarns are dyed too dark this will also change the colour of the overall tapestry background. Remember, warp threads lay on top of the in-laid wool and if the colour is different between those two materials the background will tend to change drastically tending to make it much darker -- so be careful how dark you dye your warp yarns.

A novice fibre artist may need or wish to add additional horizontal or vertical lines, further dividing a set of square blocks into a number of scales to be followed even more closely by the artist (picture 39). These scales must also be identical in size with one another.

Pictures 40 and 41. As the inlaying of the tapestry is advancing the drawing of the cartoon becomes easier because one can now follow the weave distinct sharp lines into the cartoon to be followed in the warp threads.

Picture 42. As the weaving process continues, wool particles tend to fall off as the in-laying of wool continues. Therefore, it is necessary

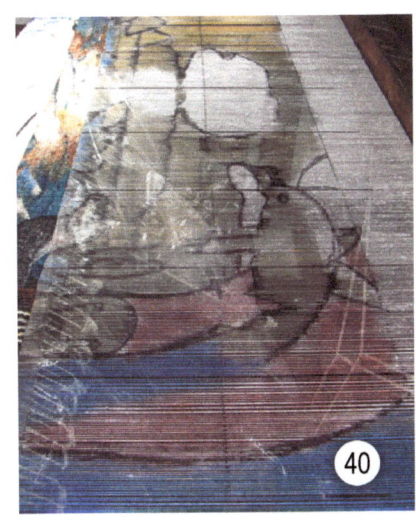

to place a protective plastic sheet under and over the warp yarns in order to avoid dirt and other particles from falling on the tapestry itself. It is also advisable to place another plastic sheet by the front bar and over the tapestry. This way sweat or dirt from your hand will not stain the already woven tapestry.

Warp yarns must be in a neutral position when either dyeing or transferring the cartoon. This means that the heddle and reed are in an even balance which helps with the dyeing and transferring process. One of the two peddles is kept under tension while the in-laying wool is in process. The tension bar (which is located between the two peddles) is to hold in place one peddle while the in-laid process continues. Changing position of the peddles takes place each time a weft thread is passed. In other words, when the weft process is finished one or the other peddle remains fixed in place until a complete scale is in-laid thus a new position of the peddle continues as a new weft is passed.

Life-sized cartoons can be directly transferred onto the warp yarn by placing the paper between the warp threads. Simply re-position the heddles which will direct the warp threads onto an even level of closure. Thus, the cartoon will remain in a fixed position. Following that, you could directly trace both the outline and the details directly onto the warp. When finished, simply create a shed with your warp yarn remove your cartoon page. You now have your cartoon inscribed onto the warp yarn.

Chapter 8
PREPARING YOUR WARP THREADS

PREPARING YOUR WARP THREADS

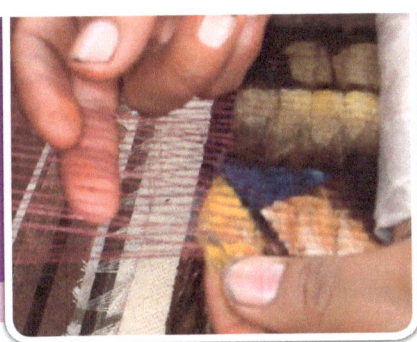

PREPARING YOUR WARP THREADS

Pictures 45, 46, 47. Carefully pass warp threads through the reed. Tie warp yarn in groups of 6 onto the warp bar at the front beam. Make sure you have an even tension as you tie them onto the warp bar.

To avoid waste of warp yarn (normally tied onto the cloth beam located below) you can use a strong cord secured onto the warp bar over both the front beam and at the bottom where the cloth beam is located.

Pictures 49, 50, 51, 52. Once tension is established, you can begin to weave the plain weave to about 5 cm in width. This plain weave should be done with the same warp yarn. On picture 110 you see the curve of the weft yarn. This

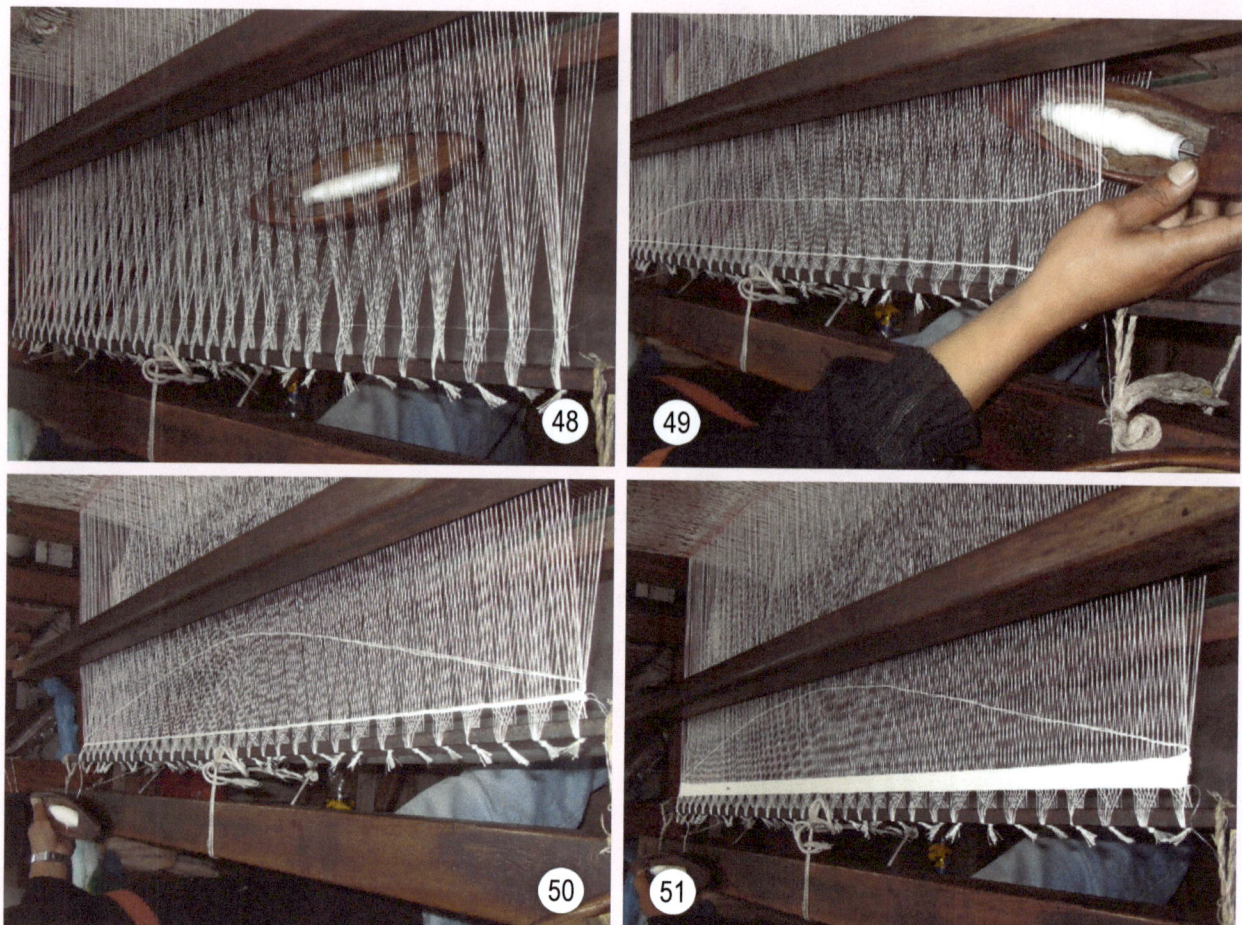

is done in order to avoid disruptive tension of the weft passing which will cause intake in the selvedge of the tapestry. With this method there will be no in-take and the plain weave will remain its proper size.

In the in-laid wool process, tones and shades are achieved by finger-carding different colours of wool [i.e. a medium tone of brown can be achieved in mixing (hand-carding) a dark with lighter tone of brown]. The percentage of one colour over the other must be practiced as you go along. Pay attention to the design's requirement of colours or tones and do the mixing (finger-carding) accordingly. Maintain as close a colour mixing as possible for better results. As you can see in pictures 50 to 51, the plain weave is in place and the warp yarn is dyed in accordance to the design's requirement.

FINGER CARDING

Finger-carded wool is shown in picture 52. Small portions of wool are removed from the rolag. The amount of finger-carded wool separated from the rolag should be about the thickness of your thumb. The length would depend on the design space you are about to in-lay in the scale. Finger-carding and mixing is the process by which you entwine two or more colours to create a specific aesthetic background. Similarly, for a large space of background in the scale, it is best to finger-card correspondingly large quantities of wool of required colours. This process of finger-carding wool is a single task repeated every time you take a portion of wool out of the rolag to be in-laid into the tapestry.

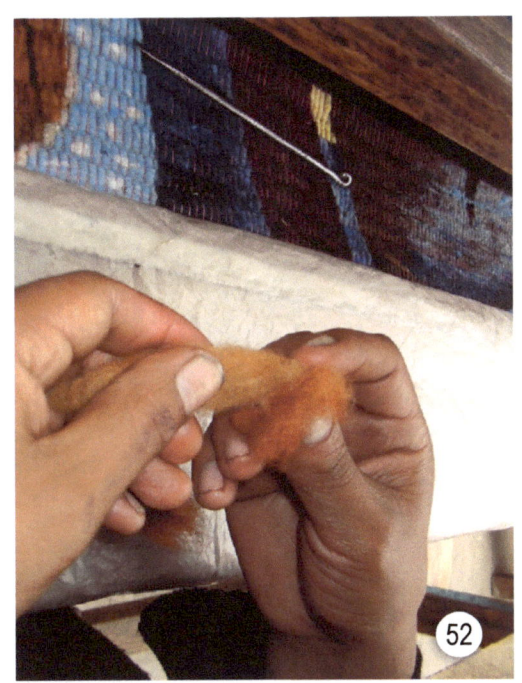

Pictures 53, 54. Depth of a two-toned shade if required as a background or for a specific localized tone will be always finger-carded to a correct mixture of colours. Use your finger as a carder to take apart (or mix) both colours to create a unique shade or tone. A clouded sky, for example, would require a light and dark blue or light blue with white, depending on the effect you wish to create. Another example to ponder is a water reflection of a blue sky. It may require the finger-carding of green mixed with blue to represent alkaline in the water and blue for the sky. The percentage of the amount of each colour will depend on the design's requirement and on your skills to mix those appropriately.

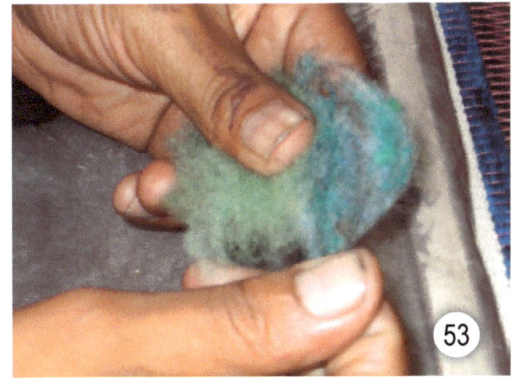

It should be noted that while the colours of the rolag hanging over the beater bar are representing general colours, it is in the finger-carding of those colours that will provide you with the final colour combination. This final stage must be done, once again, with your fingers mixing and comparing colour shades with the one in the picture or cartoon of your tapestry.

IN-LAYING WOOL

Picture 55 and 56. Lifting warp threads with your fingers will permit wool to enter the warp shed. Whether in the beginning or in the middle of each scale, it is necessary to lift the warp threads to allow easy in-laying of wool. This is a continuous process that takes place for every inch of in-laid wool. You may also use your fingers from both hands as shown on picture 56 to slide the wool in place. This process is performed many times during the making of the tapestry. So let your fingers do the work. When out of horizontal position, in-laid wool can be pushed with the aide of the beater to adjust the alignment. The use of the beater is done every time you in-lay wool and it is an integral part of the in-laid process. Once again, finger-carding uses your fingers to in-lay the wool; with the metal picker and the reed you can

position, remove and correct the task of in-laying wool process.

Picture 55 to 56. Starting from right to left, use your left hand fingers and lift up warp threads to sufficiently allow entrance of wool. You may notice how fluffy the wool appears. This is because it went through a finger-carder before being in-laid. The approximate width of normal in-laid wool is one inch; unless otherwise needed, this amount of wool is standard.

Once wool is in-laid, use both index and thumbs to slide it in place. When beginning a scale remember to leave enough overhang wool to form a strong selvedge. To finish the selvedge correctly, lift up the outside warp yarn allowing the wool to pass over and under the shed. Double up the wool under two or more bottom warp threads. This will interlock the wool within the space of each bottom warp thread. Once selvedge is in place, release warp yarn which will cause a tension between it and the wool.

It would be wrong to view the structural design, colours, shades and tones (in other words, the wave), vertically. The vertical structural build-up of in-laid wool is open to mis-structures by regarding the scale itself secondary.

Like a painter strokes, vertical build up of in-laid wool would be going against the natural flow of pictorial tapestry's scales.

Hand-Carding and Colour Mixing is a constant activity that shapes and gives colour form in the design's details. By using the metal picker to spread coloration is a mode of activity which gives direction to wool just been in-laid. The beater is also used every time you in-lay wool to position it in the horizontal level of the general scale

CREATING A DISTINCTIVE SHARP LINE

Briefly said, you can achieve a distinctive-sharp-line between two or more colours by in-laying a background first and, by doubling up the end of the next in-laid wool, you place the latter over the former where the sharp-line is needed. A third layer of wool is now needed over the 'middle' in-laid wool allowing it to show a 'line' between the background-and-the-third in-laid wool, thus sandwiching the middle layer of wool (which is the actual distinctive-sharp-line between two or more colours of wool. Study the pictures as you re-read this if you wish.

Alternatively, or to compare, distinctive-sharp-separation is achieved by first placing the background wool and inserting the next colour (doubling up its edge) just above where the separation is needed

Picture 60 shows a blue wool just being in-laid as a background to create a distinctive-sharp-line. A thin layer of darker tone is placed over and at the 'edge' of the background. With the use of the metal picker spread out the ends of the dark tone now forming a distinctive-sharp-line over the lighter-tone background.

In pictures 61 and 62, the distinctive-sharp-line is clearly defined forming a concentrated line of separation between tones and colours. This is achieved by overlapping one layer of wool over the next starting from the bottom, proceeding to

the middle and finishing at the front layer. In the upper part of picture 62, the blue, browns and buff are joined by doubling-up the ends of wool when overlapping the next (see Pictures 60, 61, 62).

Pictures 63 to 64 shows the dark line between the yellowish colour and the aforementioned other colours are placed within the scale before overlapping the yellowish tone of wool.

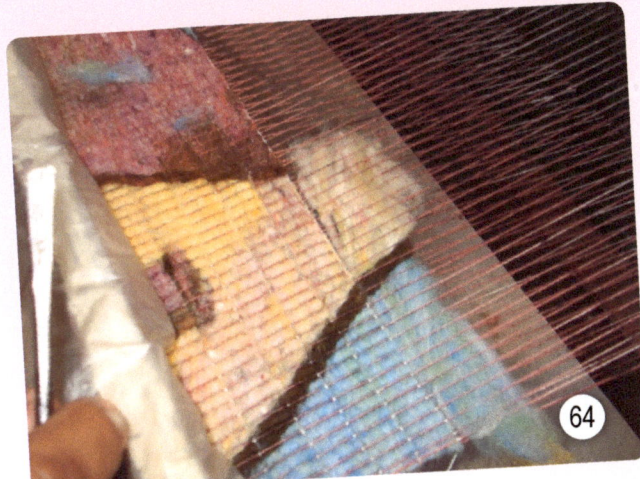

As mentioned previously, scales are built from back (background) to front by overlapping the layers of in-laid wool. In pictures 67 to 70, the dark tone wool forms the background and the subsequent yellow is in-laid overlapped and shaped by fingers and/or metal picker. Always start from the right-hand side to the left, each segment of in-laid wool overlapping in part the previous sequence of coloured in-laid wool in large or small portions.

In pictures 60 to 65, you are shown multiple in-laid wool of different colours, tones and shades with distinctive-sharp-lines and separations. Yet, the in-laid procedure remains the same. Build each scale from the right-hand-side overlaying the next layer of wool (left-hand-side), doubling edges of wool to form sharp-lines or separations; always starting from back to front (or background to foreground).

HAND-CARDING A DISTINCTIVE LINE:

All in-laid wool must be hand-carded before placed in the scale. The amount of wool placed within a scale is not an exact figure, but it must be consistent with maintaining or thickening to form a strong-built tapestry that will withstand a vertical stretch. Hand-carding wool everytime and in every step is part of the space accumulate to provide that strength. Whether you are creating a double-edge on your hand-carded wool (to become a distinctive line) or general background in-laid hand-carding of wool is a must. A 'fluffy' wool becomes easier to manipulate within the scale and move to its correct position.

PROVIDING A DISTINCT SEPARATION BETWEEN TWO COLOURS:

This applies where two of more colours without a third distinctive line between them, you must simply double-up the foremost in-laid wool and place at the edge of the bottom one. This will separate the two colours in a straight or uneven 'line' depending on your design's requirement.

As mentioned previously, weft must be passed three times to ensure that its scale is firmly fixed in place. Use strong but fine thread. Pressure must be put on the scale by using the beater against the in-laid wool every time you pass the weft. After weft is done, you may wish to check the scales ensuring even line-up and using the metal picker for any corrections (See picture 75).

TIPS

While the eye will 'travel' across the tapestry's overall view, your concentration should not be diffused all over the tapestry itself. Details constitute small parts of wool within the overall structure of the tapestry scale. While you look at the picture, as a whole, it is the horizontal scale that takes your attention, your hand-carding and mixing of colours, shades and tones that form your understanding of the relation between the previous in-laid wool to the next one that is most important. Otherwise (at most times) you'll view your practical work in terms of vertical execution rather than horizontal one. In other words, each horizontal scale should and must be in and of an end in itself, with a final result of having a well defined structure within the limitations of a scale. Do not assume how the 'scale' will look like in relation to what you are in-laying at the moment. If you do, you'll find that your 'work' has changed from horizontal to a vertical direction which would result in poor definition of the scale's internal structure. This is because, one tends to justify skipping certain fine details of the present scale, assuming and making up the details that were lost on the next above scale.

SELVEDGE PROTECTION

As the scale comes to an end, the left over in-laid wool must be secure in a place where there will be no danger of being pulled away by accident. Therefore, as you can see, in pictures 76 to 78, the wool is placed under the warp shed and is entwined within the bottom warp yarn. As the wool is placed and secured between the warp threads, it follows that in-laid wool is also interlocked by the next weft passing.

In picture 76, a plastic sheet protector is placed over the tapestry on top of tapestry to prevent dirt and hand sweat from spoiling the tapestry's colour. You can also see the tension stick at the edge of the plastic sheet which prevents in-take of tapestry selvedge.

REMOVING TAPESTRY FROM LOOM

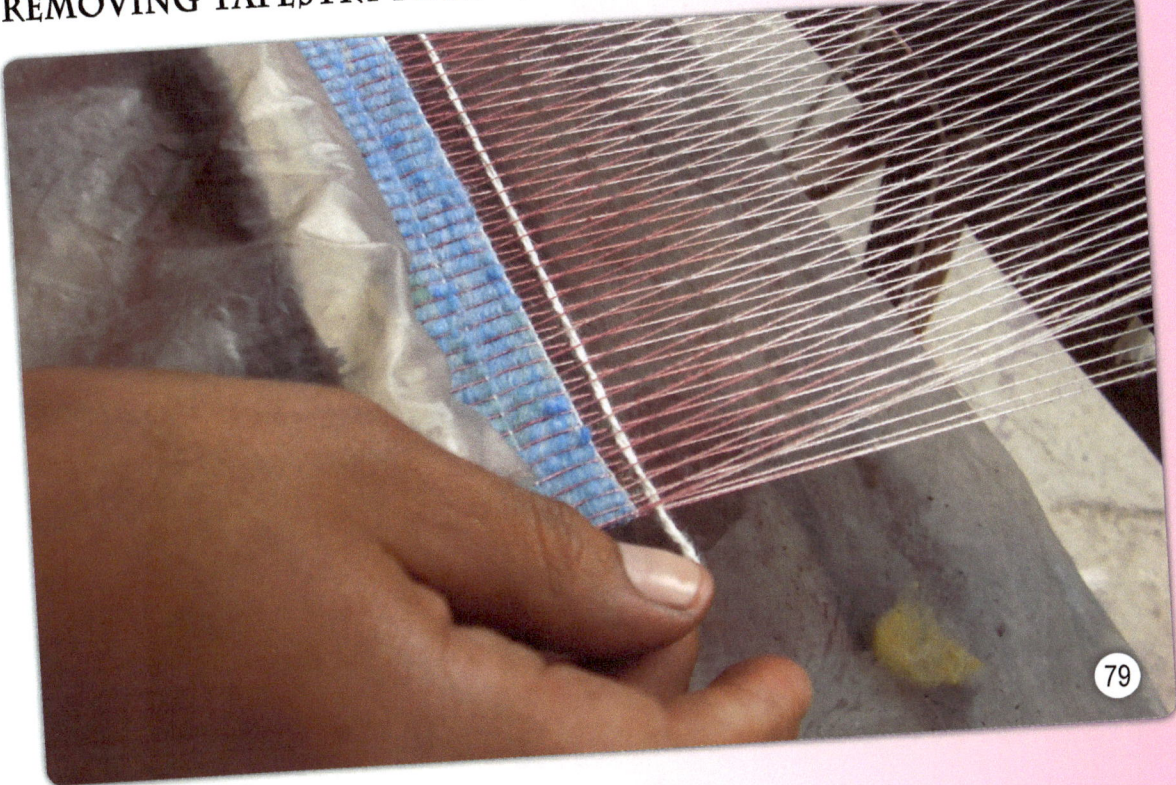

In each tapestry there are two plain weaves (one at the beginning and the other at the end of the tapestry) which secure and strengthen the tapestry itself. Once the in-laid is finished, start to weave the plain weave identical to the first one. Remember to curve your weft thread as to avoid in-take. Pictures 79 and 80 show a 5 cm of plain weave made of thick weft yarn.

Once the final plain weave is in place you can begin the process of removing the tapestry from the loom (pictures 81, 82, 83). Using sharp scissors, begin to cut a group of weft yarn and tie off in knots. Continue the process until the tapestry is free.

Remove the rest of the tapestry from the cloth bar. Cut off the rest of the knotted ties and remove the tapestry from the steel rod (picture 84).

FINISHING OFF TAPESTRY

In picture 84, the second removal of the tapestry is done at the front bar. Warp threads protruding the plain weave should now be doubled under the plain weave and sewn on to a fixed position as shown on picture 85. It is adviseable to pass a sewn thread (i.e. stitch) two or three times to make sure the plain weave is well secured to withstand any stretching pressure.

Word of Caution: do not cut off any part of the plain weave (once the tapestry is removed from the loom). If you do, the warp-tension within will pull-back the yarn and will leave the near scales of in-laid wool without any weave. Without warp-weave, the scale will simply pull apart.

CROSS WARPING: HOW TO AVOID FIGURE DISTORTION

Within any fabric done in a loom there is a balance of tension between warp and weft yarns. When this pull and push is evenly balanced the fabric does not display noticeable evidence of over or one-sided tension, no upward or downward curves at the edge of the fabric, no uneven surface when laid flat.

In-laid wool, on the other hand, has little or no resistance against uneven tension of warp and weft thread when there exists an imbalance between them. Any stress (tension) will show up in places where the warp yarn is unevenly set between others and, at this point, therefore, there will be a weak spot of

tension. Such a weakness becomes vulnerable against the pull and push of other warp yarns and the weft threads.

Such vulnerable spots tend to distort the picture when one or more sides pull more than normally should. Lines, especially those that are vertical, would appear distorted at some mid-section of the tapestry's theme. Some correction can be achieved when the tapestry is set within a fixed frame and (where the tapestry is stretched warp-wise) thus re-setting the warp yarns back to the original tension level.

A single solution to picture-distortion is to reduce overall yarn tension prior to the in-laying of wool. How you judge a warp yarn tension is a matter of experience (trial and error), and/or by the general feel when passing your hand over the warp at loom. Experience will show you what constitutes firm, medium and lax warp yarn tension feels like. Generally medium tension warping is ideal for in-laid wool.

Every tapestry contains within its theme a general area where fine details are concentrated or widespread. These areas need to be dealt with using extreme care. You must make sure that those fine details will not be distorted when the tapestry is removed from the loom. This means there exists a set tension between the warp and the weft yarn. This tension sometimes affects the overall position of details and harmony of lines.

To avoid a possible design distortion, the following steps should be taken into consideration:

a) Build your scales at the normal width of space until you arrive two scales before the area where far more intricate details are commencing. Build the next scales at the half-inch width as you approach the core area of intricacy.

b) Pass 2 instead of 3 weft passes for the next scale above. Cross warping is formed when 2 weft passes are executed for each scale in relation to the next above scale. This process is called cross-warping. In this way, the previous warp yarn would 'land' in the center of the two warps of the next scale.

Chapter 9
CREATING INTRICATE DETAILS

CREATING INTRICATE DETAILS

Pictures 89 and 91. Once in-laid wool is in place, use the metal picker to adjust its position, smoothen its surface, push downwards any piece of wool sticking above the warp yarns, pull or push away wool sections in the direction desired, or make space for the next in-laid over the top of the previous one.   On picture 96, you can see overhanging wool that needs to be folded under as well as observing the metal picker smoothening the in-laid wool shown on picture 95.

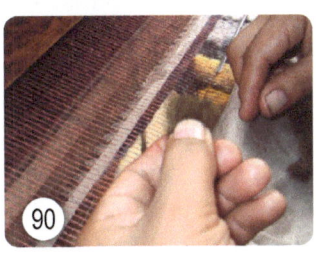

On picture 94 you see the same in-laid wool forming a space on its far left hand side. This space was made by using the metal picker to allow a brown colour wool to enter there diagonally (picture 91). The metal picker separates the brown colour wool and forms an angle to be fulfilled by the next coloured wool. This process is done within the limited space of the design itself. Remember, the building up of each segment of in-laid wool begins from back to front and from right hand side to left with the latter over-laid on top of the right to form the next sequence of in-laid process.

Picture 91. Once again, by using the metal picker, it is possible to create space for the next in-laid wool, or modify a new space.   Use the metal picker to poke, push or pull the wool as required. In this picture the metal picker is correcting the bottom blue colour wool as its edge is aligned with the top brown wool.   Therefore, whenever there is a need for any sort of correction or modification, use the metal picker. In picture 95, this is exactly what is taking place (i.e. corrections of in-laid wool). You finish the scale by creating a left-hand side selvedge.

Commencing in-laid is a simple process: whether you have a distinctive sharp line to form or an interesting over-lay background to create, you always start from back towards the front (or bottom to top). To build your theme from back to front, the process is as follows:

1. Take an adequate amount of wool from the rolag. Finger-card and bend wool edge, placing it next to the right-hand side wool to form a contrasting demarcation.

2. Finger-card the next colour wool that will over-lay on top of the contrasting demarcation allowing a certain width which will form, now, the distinct line. This distinct line can be vertical, diagonal, round, square, pointed, sharp or 'fuzzy' line, or odd-shaped. The requirements of the in-laid wool allow in difference positions, remains the same.

To form a distinct line horizontally, the process is identical:
a) Finger-card an adequate amount of wool to form your basic background.
b) Over-lay the next portion of wool (with its bent edge) and position it horizontally (from the top) in mid-section of the bottom background wool.
c) Placing the third (and final) in-laid wool (with its edge bent) slide it in position over the previous second layer allowing the desired width (of mid-section) to form a distinct line.

3. Using the metal picker correct the wool in its proper position. With smooth strokes over the in-laid wool, spread uneven surfaces as desired. Position the bent wool to the selected position (over the background) to form a distinct line.

4. Always allow the extra length of wool to permit the following one to be over-laid without showing unwanted ends.

The above process can achieve the same results whether the lines are horizontal, vertical, diagonal, or whether the separations between colours are at the edge or in the mid-section of the background in-laid wool. Square, rectangular or round shapes of in-laid wool are also achieved by the same method of doubling up the edge of the wool intended to be over-laid on the previous one. With the help of the metal picker, you smoothen the square ends (or round ones) in accordance to the design's requirement. Think one inch at a time within the horizontal scale and in-lay your theme in the same mode.

5. Uneven scale can be straightened by using the beater (before weft is passed). Beat scale to match the width of the previous one (approximately half-inch wide). Pass the first weft thread and beat hard to achieve the desired width. Second and third weft passing is repeated and the

beater is once again used to achieve the half-inch width of the scale.

6. To create a distinct separation between two colours simply in-lay your background wool first; then over-lay the second layer (with its bent end) at the required position where the separation is desired. Here you now have a separation between two colours without the delineation of a distinct line.

A lot of in-laying work requires a good eye-hand co-ordination especially when it comes to the colour mixing and the amount of wool needed for each step in the in-laying process (within its scale). It is suggested therefore to use the beater as a ruler to slightly beat the in-laid wool and also to adjust where there is a lesser amount of in-laid wool placed incorrectly. The beating should formulate a unified flow to the wool. When needed (if you detect uneven space in the scale), you may wish to add additional small amounts of wool where required.

Most in-laid wool fibre artists use the beater every single time they are in-laying wool. As such, this process completes the required step-by-step uniform scale.

In order to achieve levelling or smoothening of in-laid wool surface, place your metal picker between the wool and warp threads as shown on picture 95. With a counter-clockwise movement, the wool should remain under the warp threads. This process is repeated every single time you in-lay wool -- whether it is for a background, thinly spread as a single colour, separation between two colours, or to create a distinct line between them. The metal picker (aside from the loom itself) is the only tool you require to use for the purpose of in-laying, levelling, adding wool, correcting, and/or directing it to its proper place. Note the extra wool and the selvedge. By lifting the outside bottom warp thread pass over end wool and insert it inwards just under the bottom side of the warp shed. Once in place the doubled up wool will form an even selvedge identical to the next one shown in picture 101. Therefore, leaving extra wool over-hanging is a must in order to achieve a strong selvedge.

SPECIAL EFFECTS

However simple or intricate your in-laid tapestry is, the practical steps to achieve a successful transfer of an image onto a fibre art still remains the same; you always begin with the further-most background. All other details are added from the base (towards you) -- whether those details are in the center or at the edge of such background. In other words, read your image from back to front.
Let us analyze the photographs 97 and 98.

1. A solid white background depicts a reflection of clouds on water. Note that (from right to left) as the brownish colour approaches the white there is a blue colour separating the brown, blue and white. At the edge, the brown lies on top of the colour blue then the colour white, thus allowing the blue to show a certain amount of its colour to effectively separate all three colours.

2. Light blue colour wool is hand-carded with white to give a mixed effect of both colours. Here, the light blue colour of in-laid wool lies on top of the white background.

3. In this case, the further-most background of brown is showing through the white and blue foreground colours. Looking towards the far right, you can see that the blue colour wool has been 'lightly' in-laid over the top of the mixture of the deep and the light brownish colour. The mixture of browns are in-laid first (forming the background) with the light blue in-laid sparingly. Space is created with the use of the metal picker to separate colours.

4. This distinctive-sharp-line of black colour separates brown from dark blue. Beginning from right to left, brown (representing the island terrain) is in-laid first. The black, therefore, is in-laid at the edge of the brown colour allowing (allocating space) for the next in-lay of dark blue.

5. From right to left, the blue forms the background. Next the brown colour (with a doubled up edge) forms a distinctive-line-of-separation between the brown and the blue colours. The blue to the left is then in-laid on top of the edge of the brown colour.

6. This segment represents an interesting combination of multiple in-laid wool colours. The further-most background (to the right) is the dark brown. Next the light brownish (forms the background) for the sparingly light blue colour on top. Within the light blue you can see a spectrum of white forming a reflection of blue sky.

NOTE:
You may wish to take the opportunity to analyze the colour sequence of the 'ground' on the island. Remember all uneven edges are done with a smooth, roundish movement of the metal picker forming hair-like edges.

IN-LAID BODY DETAILS

In Pictures 99 to 107 in general, most detail in tapestry is done during a normal process of weaving. Additional required details are in-laid when the scale in semi-completed. Such details are added before the weft is done and are placed between the warp yarn, and on the surface of the already in-laid wool. Those are secured by the interlock of warp and weft yarns.

Some superfine details are difficult to place in the tapestry's body and are even harder to hold and finger-card due to their small size. Most superfine details are needed to be placed in an exact position within the overall theme of the tapestry. For example, a pupil of an eye, a star in the night sky, an animal's hoof or the shade of a person's face or any other important detail can be still added after the scale is completed and interlocked in place.

With the aide of the metal picker you can guide small amounts of wool and, by poking, pushing and pulling, you can place in the exact position needed. The angled tip of the metal picker can lift up a warp yarn with enough space to permit the entrance and positioning of a superfine detail.

With a little patience, the task of adding superfine details can be achieved. Those details can, sometimes, make

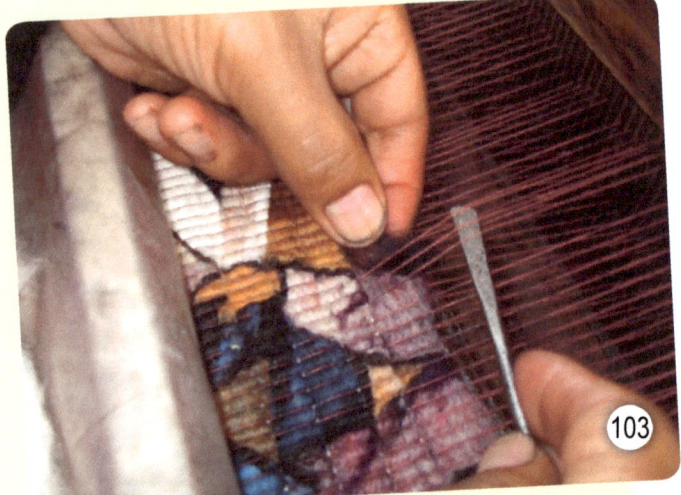

the difference between a fine intricate Pictorial Tapestry and a good quality one.

Starting with mixing and/or hand-carded wool of the appropriate amount … The first layer of in-laid wool is the back most one which would form the theme's background. It is placed, adjusted and beaten with the reed lightly into its position and spread with the metal picker.

A second layer of in-laid hand-carded wool would form the middle layer to form wither a separate or a distinctive line between two more colours.

Third and subsequent layers of wool (placed on top of the middle and background ones) will constitute the finer details of the tapestry's theme. Special attention should be placed to follow the different shades, tones and 'structure' of shapes and lines. It is these details that would show most distinctively once the tapestry theme is created. Do not exclude any type of detail – this would separate a well done tapestry from a mediocre one.

PRACTICE, PRACTICE, PRACTICE:

Things are easier said than done. Practise what is being shown in this book. Practise with small segments of in-laid wool in different styles of forms, shapes, colours, shades and tones. Themes are not important (for this moment). Techniques would lead you to a state of accumulation of experience, and practice will become your perfection.

Remember, if you just in-lay a segment of wool that does not fit in the representation you are trying to create, you can always remove it from the scale, correct it, re-direct it, re-shape it, thin spread it (or concentrate it) in its correct position. Keep your

concentration on the picture grate (cartoon), for direction; keep also, in your mind's 'eye', the general perspective of the theme you want to create. Try mixing different tones to achieve a desired background or a fine detail to be over-in-laid. Practice, practice, practice is your key to success as a fibre artist. Study the in-laid wool segments shown in pictures 99 to 107.

ADDING HORIZONTAL LINES:

Adding horizontal, vertical, curved lines, and other superfine details is part of an intricate tapestry's theme. Most of the above requirements are in-laid over a multi-colour background. First you must in-lay the background and secure it in its proper position.

Next, make a string-like wool yarn in the palms of your hand (lifting the warp thread with a metal picker) in-lay it on top of the background wool just under the warp threads.

In the case of a 'dot' (an eye for example) you may in-lay it in its correction position and (again with the help of a metal picker) push dot downwards enough to secure the 'eye' in a fixed position.

In picture 108, the horizontal line has just been in-laid and directed (109) with the help of the metal picker to its correct position (110 and 111).

This technique can be used to add dots, eyes, squares, triangles and anything that is far too small to be handled by hands only. Remember, place the background first, then the fine detail over-laid and adjust it with the metal picker.

Chapter 10
THE BUSINESS OF YOUR FIBRE STUDIO

THE BUSINESS OF YOUR FIBRE STUDIO

MARKETING YOUR PICTORIAL TAPESTRY

I've always said that if you have an idea that would make you a success, give it 10 years to succeed. We all know someone who has spent many a year looking for a short cut to success. This is a complete waste of time. Most 'overnight' success stories were achieved by people who had spent many years perfecting their art.

The passage of time, as a process, is more important than strategizing for success. Take bold steps to make your in-laid Pictorial Tapestry an artwork; get it out for the public to see it; do what you have to, so that everyone will have a chance to admire your artistic creation. You must prove to both the collectors and diversified galleries that you are serious about your fibre artwork and that you are here for the long run. You are passionate tapessier artist, you are here committed. You are here to stay. Nothing will stop you from proving yourself as a tapessier. In other words, you must establish your credibility as a serious fibre artist.

The initial responsibility to succeed as an *excellent* tapessier lies with you. The first thing you must learn is to treat your studio of in-laid Pictorial Tapestry as a business! Set up your studio's artworks as a business, and run it with **operative business procedures.**

This does not diminish your artistic integrity, by any means, for there is nowhere that states that you must be, and remain, a "bohemian starving artist". Treating your studio as a business simply makes your road to the future a focused objective, sets it in your mind, and helps you to steer away from aimless drifting. Otherwise, if you just want to be a purist and and weave full time in peace and quiet in your studio, and live the life in pure artistic creative harmony, I hope you have a rich relative to support you!

Undertaking the life of a successful tapessier may be complex, but the success is attainable and within your reach.

Eventually, one day, all your efforts begin to fall into place and you gain a sense of how the whole process fits together. You feel empowered. The mystery of how to become successful tapessier begins to clear up. This is why you too must first go through life's trenches and learn the lessons so important to any tapessier's successful career.

Through this book we've traveled a long way together. I hope that I have installed in you the idea of respect for the fibre *artwork* of in-laid Pictorial Tapestry: an artwork! **Not a craft!!**

As a friend and a mentor through this book, I offer you an encouragement. I wish you luck and hope you will triumph!!

THE IDEAL BUSINESS LOCATION

The following are general recommendations for you to consider. The first obvious question we must ask is this; from what location are you going to operate your studio? To begin with, you can set up a floor loom in your apartment, home, or basement, even your bedroom will suffice. However, if you have a ground level house available, check with the local authorities to see if you can obtain a home-base business permit from your residence and if other requirements regulate setting up a studio; providing a Pictorial Tapestry studio is what you have in mind.

Attracting potential buyers and then selling them tapestries, becomes an art in itself. An open public studio to be worthwhile and profitable must follow several established rules. Catch the attention of walking traffic. Engaging visuals, such as an attractive sign, will direct the attention of the passerby out of the street and into your studio. Make this a selling environment as enticing as possible.

Make your visitors feel comfortable, greet them, and offer to answer questions: be hospitable. Have a small portable loom with a half done inlaid tapestry close by for the visitor to see the making of your fibre artwork in progress. If the loom attracts the visitor's attention, try not to get overly technical! If you have a problem relating to people (or making conversation) talk about your tapestry at hand.

Be sure that at least several finished pictorial tapestries are clearly in prominent sight displayed in what might be an approximate setting of a fibre-gallery. Pictorial tapestries that are hanging on walls must be properly lighted, and separated from one another. Do not surround them by a cluster of utility crafts such as scarves, gloves and sweaters etc. Some viewers may choose to view up close these items. Others may have trouble appreciating or understanding how a hanging Pictorial Tapestry might look at home or office setting when other artifacts nearby obstruct them. Remember to include similar weavings, per setting, and leave an adequate space between them.

Offer pictorial tapestries in all sizes and price range. A small initial sale, a simple tapestry, may lead into a much more intricate and expensive one later. Of course, for the most part, visitors attend fibre and diversified studios to buy modestly priced tapestries or even find bargains. Be aware that those visitors who tend to spend a lot more money also know what they want -- perhaps a commissioned in-laid Pictorial Tapestry from a tapessier they already know. As for those visitors who may be sitting on the fence about whether or not to buy one of your tapestries, offer them a variety of low price choices.

Have promotional material available for the taking; these do not need to be expensive prints. If you make computer printouts on gloss paper, one with more pictures than words, place those in your local tourist bureau, local hotels and/or restaurants -- and anywhere visitors might be located. Do not forget to include your location (even a small map for direction), your phone number, your website, and the studio's hours. Your number one goal is to bring the public into your studio and make as many sales as possible. Consider taking a down payment to hold the tapestry until it is paid in full.

Offer for a low fee or **rent** a Pictorial Tapestry **(but NEVER NEVER NEVER** for free) to reputable hotels and restaurants in your area. Have the establishment include (in writing) in their insurance policy the full retail value of your tapestries. Get a letter of confirmation from the insurance company.

Do not sell yourself short; explain to restaurateurs and hotels why your tapestries will make their establishment more attractive to locals and visitors. Do not let some local business person(s) make you think 'they' are doing you a favour having your pictorial tapestries in their place of business. It is your tapestries that will be beautifying their places, and for that alone they must pay for this privilege. As such, you believe in yourself and your fibre artwork, and are confident about the value of your accomplishments.

Remember that you are creating beautiful inlaid pictorial tapestries that bring a joy into your life, and selling them brings joy into the life's of others. Renting them brings joy to the public at large, and at the same time, you make money!! Now that's success!!

YOUR STUDIO AS YOUR FIBRE GALLERY

Most fibre art collectors choose to shop exclusively through direct contacts. Collectors feel that they can get a better price, experience the representation and have more direct answers to their questions about the Pictorial Tapestry itself. Here are some points for you to consider;

- Keep regular business hours, just like any other local business in your area. Display the hours of operation and have them during accepted business hours. Also, advise potential customers that you are available by appointment or after hours on certain days.
- During visiting hours make your visitors feel comfortable by having low music, (as background) avoiding silence which can make buyers reluctant to speak. Answer questions with politeness and show them what they want to see. Do not load them with promotional material as they are not there to read.
- Keep your explanations simple. By this I mean, do not lecture them and make them feel un-cultured or become argumentive with them. Above all, do not tell them the story of your life, your travels, and of your famous friends.
- If collectors with modest budgets show interest in a tapestry of their choice, respond positively. Do not try to sell them another more expensive one.
- If potential collectors cannot make up their minds which tapestry would look good in their office or home, offer to take it to the location to try it out. This offer would more indebt them to you. Consider extending these sorts of courtesies.
- In your gallery, have prices on display by placing a small card next to each tapestry, so that your visitors can view them simultaneously. Most collectors feel uncomfortable asking the sale price of a given tapestry. You can also offer them a price catalogue.
- Consider keeping a tapestry on 'hold' until is paid in full, and promote 'alternative purchase options'. Offer free delivery within your area, city or a prescribed distance from your studio.

- Make sure to set aside the most visual part of your studio from the street as your fibre gallery. As a rule, the more you can display (without clutter) the better.
- Pay attention to the tourist trade and create tapestries that are easily placed in a small vehicle. Look around you; ask yourself, what attracts tourists in your area? Is it fishing, skiing, or some particular event? How about creating a Pictorial Tapestry that reflects that particular event? Imagine a spectacular salmon flying out of the water either to catch a fly or by the hook of a fisherman? How about keeping a calendar of events in your area, and changing your fibre art and your gallery setting to reflect those events?
- Use your studio gallery wisely; you may wish to offer space to other quality tapessiers to sell their fibre art works and/or invite other weavers to use your location to display their utility products (especially around Christmas and holiday times). This may be your 'daily bread and butter'.
- Avoid having friends, relatives, and colleagues use your studio (during regular business hours) as a drop-in center. It is inopportune when you are in the middle of a possible sale or in a time when a potential customer is trying to make up his/her mind about buying a pictorial tapestry.

TURN YOUR STUDIO INTO A CLASSROOM

Teaching one weekend workshop to both adult and children (10 to 18) is a way to earn an extra income, and to increase your effectiveness as a teacher of inlaid tapestry. Here are some suggestions:

- Make a sign that says 'Art School of Pictorial Tapestry'.
- Invest in 6 – 12 small frame looms and have enough wool supplies in as many colours. Have a number of cartoon designs that could be made into small 12"x12"

tapestries. Make sure that a beginner could finish a small tapestry by the time the workshop is over.
- Choose no more than 6-8 students per workshop; if you have more you may wish to split the group for morning and later classes.
- You may wish to use your larger loom, with you at the loom bench with the rest of the students standing; this way they could all see you doing your work.
- Charge your students a fee that *would include* the wool supplies. Set a minimum of hours for workshopping; depending on the student's age, they tend to have different spans of attention. If short workshops become popular, why not consider a full day or full weekend version combined with other events and lunch to go along.
- As a tapessier, set a goal to teach other weavers or fibre artists; this way you can widen your networking. Fibre artists who learn from you would share information about in-laid pictorial tapestries with perhaps their weaver's association, and/or possible future show participants. All of whom would tend to purchase their supplies from you.
- As a tapessier, you will find that by maintaining contact with other fibre artists, weavers, and dyers, you are more effective at creating and marketing your artwork than doing it alone.
- Add your student's names to a mailing list for future workshops, gallery shows and open studios. You'll find that students tend to return for shows, as well as, for additional workshops. These visitors often bring their friends and family who might possibly be interested in learning the art of in-laid tapestry.
- Selling your tapestries is another advantage of teaching workshops in your fibre studio. Make sure to display a good selection of your tapestries while the events are ongoing. Remember, your students see your selection of tapestries all the while they are learning.

- During the course of the workshop these students find out a bit more about how your tapestries are made, and come to understand them on an additional skill level than the one they have at present. As these students become more familiar with the art of in-laid pictorial tapestries, they will feel less intimidated, more comfortable, and more inclined to purchase one if they like it.
- It is said, that the more you teach the more you learn. Workshops are a great way to gain experience and improve both your skills and the ability to speak about in-laid tapestries in public. As time goes on, your public speaking can lead to engagements as a guest or resident tapessier at colleges, adult or continuing education programs, schools and teaching workshops in other cities.
- A day workshop should run from 4-6 hours. Charge the going minimum hourly wages in your area; for example, if the minimum hourly wage is $7.75 x 6 = $46.50 (make it $50) per student. For 8 students, your one day workshop will bring you $400 for 6 hours.
- If you are planning a two day workshop (for, say, graduates of the previous workshop), do the same calculation, that is, a total of 12 hours of teaching; this time, add 10% to include the wool supplies. At 20% additional charge (all inclusive), you may wish to provide your students with home cooked meals as part of your program. This will create a luxurious and nourishing atmosphere. Short breaks and snack breaks should be included in the schedule but not the lunch break.
- Special attention must be paid to the following: the two most important criteria for successful workshops are that a simple but complete method or technique be taught in the one full day or full weekend period, and that each student come away with a finished in-laid of a simple tapestry. This gives students a feeling of accomplishment and mastery. A number of small frame looms, already

set up with the base plain weave will be enough for a day or two-day workshop, and lets the student achieve a simple design.

- Decide what you want to teach, for both adult and children, and plan your schedule ahead of time. Inlaid the design yourself in order to make sure that your students can accomplish the desired project within the set period of time.
- Announce the up coming workshop weeks ahead of time. Advertise that no experience is necessary in order to attend. Indicate that experienced weavers who sign up will be able to learn something new. That way you maximize the number of potential students. You should know how to address a variety of skills levels and still make sure that your students feel comfortable and accomplish something.
- Place a computer print advertisement (with tapestry picture), in places where weavers, craftsmen, and people who like art in general congregate. These include public libraries, bulletin boards, weavers' associations and their newsletters, recreation centres, fibre art centres, art schools, colleges, cafes and coffee shops in your area, community associations and galleries, local theatre groups and active senior centres. Always, print a colour picture of an inlaid tapestry on your printed material: remember a picture of a simple design is worth a thousand words.
- Determine what supplies are needed and provide everything yourself (usually the best option). All a student has to do is present themself. Just remember to include supply cost into your overall fee.
- Plan for having the number of students you think is worth your maximum. Large numbers would be difficult in a short time, especially when you have to jump from one loom to another -- unless you have a helper to assist you.

- Advanced teaching of in-laid Pictorial Tapestry, (for those students who have successfully completed lower levels), is another option to explore as experienced weavers may also express a desire to learn. At this level of teaching, for a weekend workshop, the cost per student should be no less than $350 including material.

USING MUSIC

There are many reasons to necessitate using background music in a day long or weekend workshops.

Background music, as people arrive at your fibre studio, helps to create a welcoming environment. Remember, your students, most likely, have never met each other and may be self-concious. The point is to avoid a "doctor's waiting room syndrome" where everyone sits quietly, speaking only in hushed tones or whispers. In this case music acts as friendly 'neutral noise' allowing students to talk more freely and to interact. You may wish to use an upbeat music at a low-to-moderate volume that will offend no one, even at the risk of being 'too easy listening' like jazz.

However, while you are lecturing, there should be no music. Only during hands–on excercises music can be used to good effect. Generally, choose a non–vocal over a vocal music as words can be disruptive to some people's thinking process of concentration. Of course, if the practical session is creative and fairly noisy then its less of an issue. Increase music volume from low to moderate depending on activity.

In breaks, music is a welcome 'white noise' in the same way, for it allows students to chat freely without self–conciousness. It is far harder to break a silence than talk within white noise and students feel less 'overheard' when talking against background music, even if it is not loud enough to mask their conversation.

Of course, one cannot avoid students' personal preferences with music. If you can choose upbeat music, it is more likely (and condusive) to be happy than sad.

The aim is to maintain a level of energy at all times. Pay attention to spending too long on one practical point, or an activity that's long and passive. It can drop the level of student's energy and suppressing their willingness to participate and even sending some of them to sleep.

As a toe-in-the-water testing, review your day/session and ensure that the energy level is high enough to offer changes before adding in the breaks and scheduling energy boosters.

Further brief suggestions may include:
Give a very brief introduction of who you are, your fibre artistic background, the day's step by step project, the need for cell phone silence, where the toilet(s) and fire exit(s) are, and roughly how many breaks are ahead. Do not attribute times to each practice you plan before lunch break. This will give you maximum flexibility in the event of shorter or longer than planned practice and frees you from being distracted by process changes. Finally, one of the cardinal rules for keeping an energetic workshop is to be facilitative and interactive; that is, follow the 70/30 rule, 70% practice and 30% teaching.

MEDIA EXPOSURE OF YOUR STUDIO

Someone who has accepted the hard facts of advertising once said: "I know that half of the money I spend on advertising is wasted. I just don't know which half."

The best advice that I can offer you is not to plunk down large sums of money for *any* sort of advertising. It is like pouring your money down the drain. While I am in favour of publishing, I am not in favour of advertising. Why? Because the day *after* your ad is printed, it is no longer relevant to anyone. Having said this, let me proceed to give you an example from my experience:

As it happened to me, there will always be an advertising sales person who, in order to gain a hefty commission, will promise you the moon, instant success, fame and fortune from various degrees of radio and print exposure.

As it happened to me, they will try to extract money from you in exchange for such a promise. Well let me tell you this: fame and fortune comes to you from the fine fibre artwork you can create, and as such, you must *earn* your fortune! No matter how much you are willing to, as I said, plunk down for advertising, there are no 'overnight successes' nor is there an easy way to make your name known. The best road to good publicity is to go after more genuine modes of promoting your fibre artwork, all for a modest budget.

Here are some suggestions:

- Avoid 'free' websites for advertising all kinds of 'arts'; they tend to cluster cheap and irrelevant advertisements in the same page your fine inlaid tapestry is exposed.
- Participate in one-of-a-kind shows (or share a booth with another fibre artist of quality).
- Print postcards of your most popular in-laid pictorial tapestries and display them in your studio, at shows, etc. Supply them to your local gift shops (that sell tourist post cards) at cost or for a modest price. Include at the bottom of your website, your e-mail, phone number. Offer in-laid pictorial tapestries on commission.
- As was previously suggested, you may also wish to place your brochures at the tourist bureau (for free), train, bus depot and ferry terminals which are often next to other tourist attractions.
- Make sure that your inlaid tapestries are well know within your community, town or city, through networking with other fibre artists whose careers are advanced.

Think of your studio as the sun, and everything that you do outside of your studio must involve and revolve around your studio's fixed base.

Print your business cards as a miniature of your postcards and always carry them with you.

Create a consumer friendly website with different pictorial tapestries and prices, an optional payment system (i.e. PayPal), and include an order form and how to contact you. Link your website with as many weaver's associations and other fibre galleries in exchange for their link to your site.

Another way to promote yourself is to 'blow your own horn' in weavers' and fibre sites, chat rooms, and blogs by commenting on another's fine fibre work. Identify yourself as an in-laid tapessier, from (your town) and your website. This networking in discussion groups, other fibre trade magazines and weaver's publications informs editors and others of this exciting new style of tapestry. Offer yourself for interviews. Include a post card of your tapestry with your cover letter.

Do not become overly aggressive or intimidating with anyone whom you'll deal with. Let your promotion strategy take its effect throughout a reasonable frame of time. Let me tell you a true story:

I had just finished a 6'x4' tapestry (and I decided not to wait for the world to discover me), and so I took my tapestry to an art editor from a large circulation newspaper in Ontario, Canada. I managed somehow to enter the building, pass the security at the front desk, get into the elevator (all the way up to the 7th floor), there asking people to point to me the desk of the art editor. When I found him (poor fellow) he was taking a nap at his desk, sealed from sight by his cubicle wall. As I was standing in front of him, while deciding if I should wake him or not, he just then opened his eyes. He saw me standing in front of him and he was so surprised that the poor guy almost had a heart attack! Needless to say, I was never called back for an interview nor did I get a promotional article from his paper.

Remember never, never, never, pay for any type of advertising that links article content to a paid promotion. Even if a salesperson from a magazine suggests this, **don't do it.** If he promises you that the next magazine issue will contain an article about you and your artwork (and have a full colour display to boot) just simply refuse. Those who read articles about any sort of fibre art related issues are not stupid, and they will have little problem recognizing the buy-an-ad-get-an-article-for-free is an effect. Simply put, you do not want to destroy your reputation.

USING THE INTERNET

It is beyond the scope of this book to go into an indepth analysis of the effectiveness of the Internet as a medium to sell your in-laid pictorial tapestries. The first question you should ask yourself is; what is the real reason that I want a website? Do you want to provide information to everyone about in-laid pictorial tapestries, to your potential clients, as to the location of your studio, about you as a fibre artist, or about how the public can contact you to purchase a tapestry? If your plan is as simple as that, I say go for it! Remember that you are a tapessier, an artist, any idea you may have that by links the world of internet to you to capture the world of fibre art, will be a futile attempt and a good way to waste a lot of money. **WHY?** Because you are a hand producer of in-laid pictorial tapestries not a manufacturer of 'trinkets' that you can peddle from a conveyor belt.

Here are some things to consider:

- Hire a professional webpage designer who is willing to listen to you that you can work with.

- Do not put 'all your eggs in one basket'; make your website work for you *in conjunction with* the traditional ways of getting your fibre art out in the market. Show it in juried and non-juried expositions etc., and connect your artwork with diversified reputable galleries and/or agents.

- Personalize your website; make it feel like an extension of your actual studio not just another lifeless sterile site.

- Keep things simple, but provide all essential information about yourself: your complete studio address, phone number, fax and e-mail address.

- Do not give your potential clients, galleries, and museums the impression that you are secretive by showing only your email address and not telling them where you are located.

- When it comes to a website: keep it fast, easy, and well organized.

- Do not make your website appear far too complex -- like a medieval castle maze!

- Make sure that every page on your site is linked back to your home page. Contact information with your physical address should be included. Have an ordering cart and suggest visits to your studio for more selection.

- Above all, do not force your visitors to join, register, require a password or fill out any kind of questionnaire in order to access your website.

- Avoid gimmicks like special effects and complex visuals, for most of your visitors want to see your in-laid pictorial tapestries as quickly and easily as possible.

- Do not show too many tapestries "**SOLD**": do not underestimate the public's intelligence, for they tend to be suspicious about your motives, and collectors who are looking for unique fibre art will not trust you.

- Offer your tapestry art in 3, 4, and, 5 star (*) categories with related price per category. Collectors who have never bought from you before, or are not familiar with the art of inlaid tapestries, may get a bit discouraged when your tapestries cost more than they are willing to pay.

- Remember to price every piece of tapestry you have shown for sale, both on each web page and in your visual studio. Collectors, whether on the Internet or not, traditionally prefer to shop for tapestries in the privacy of their home. They want to know how much it would cost them ahead of time. They tend to be reluctant to ask for prices thinking that the tapessier will try to sell them something else.

- In your section 'visit studio for more selection' include a short page "*Tapessier's Statement*". Write about yourself as a fibre artist, in the first-person. Do not write about the aid disaster in Africa, Katrina, or how you were inspired by the seal hunt and became vegetarian **'OUCH'**. Hear me out. Collectors want to know or are more interested to know why you do what you do, and why you became a tapessier. Have your picture with your floor loom present while you are addressing your clients, it's like they are getting to know you as a real person -- by connecting an artist's face with your statement. They are more likely to buy than people who don't make the connection. Do not over do it.

- With your 'tapessier's statement', broadcast your latest artwork or fibre exposition rather that a whole lot of text.

- Do not be tempted to over 'link' with all kinds of 'artistic' websites promising you the world. As a general rule, websites are nothing more than another method of advertising, and pay-to-join or throwing links into the mix, can be costly and unproductive. Becoming one of thousands, makes you kind of like a flea on a dog (hard to find) while hoping against all odds that somehow these websites will bring you exposure and more.

- You must view your website as the extension of the yellow pages which provides collectors who are looking for a tapestry or wall hanging (or fibre art) by a quicker method of viewing your art and getting in touch with your studio.

- Regardless what these 'artistic' website (advertisers) or printing advertisers promise you, they cannot make people visit your website or your studio. Having said that, the Internet is an important marketing tool albeit with a set of limitations embodied in its marketing scope i.e., manufacturing production vs. hand-made fibre artworks.

- Look for websites that congregate people who are looking to buy a fibre artwork, a tapestry or wall hanging. You get a bigger R.O.I. (return for your investment) by selling on Ebay. I say this because the users of Ebay, in general, are buyers not lookers. Ebay is a more economical way to advertise. You will learn what works. You'll exactly see how many visitors will visit your own website and how many potential bidders you attract.

- On Ebay make sure that your fibre art is located under an appropriate category not just under "art" or "craft", because these terms include everything from native prints, photography, carpets, wall hangings, flea market junk, store bought posters, Japanese brush paintings, prints, carvings, ceramics, to origami.

- On Ebay use the title line (the most important part of your fibre art's online auction listing) to the fullest extent. Pack your limited space available with as many keywords as possible.

- On Ebay your keywords for your artworks may appear as: tapestry (ies), wall hanging(s), fibre, wool, art of the loom, woven art, weaved product(s), wall rug(s), wall covering(s), warp and weft products, pictorial weaves, Pictorial Tapestry, etc. Try different combinations of keywords. Be aware that fibre works appeal to more than one type of collector, so make sure your keywords take all such collectors into account.

- Avoid wasting space by using unrelated words on your auction listing. Collectors hardly ever 'type' words such as "exclusive", "famous", "rare", "hard to find" into search engines when looking for in-laid pictorial tapestries.

- Unless you have a permanent website store on Ebay, timing your auction is very important. Starting on Friday to the next week's Sunday (10 days), is the best time to catch bidders at home and available (the most important shopping days being Friday, Saturday, Sunday (next week's), Monday, Friday, Saturday and Sunday). Best shopping hours are during the early to mid evening hours.

- Display images, size and pertinent details of your pictorial tapestries, show a close up of Symbolic Signature, Title, and Name. A high quality image of your fibre artwork help sell your tapestries and net a much higher price.

- Do not forget to include your website in printed promotional matter for those collectors who may be interested in viewing more tapestries, and include both e-mail and physical address to write you.

- Remember that there are more free websites available to you. Yahoo.com. Amazon.com, and Google are the most popular currently.

PROMOTING YOURSELF AND STUDIO BY NETWORKING

Allow me to indulge, for a moment, to be somewhat abstract here. Let us say that you are meeting someone of a certain social status for the first time, and your focus is to convince this person to give you his/her attention as a fine tapessier. The initial probability of misinterpreting each other's expectations is far greater in the first encounter than in the second or subsequent meetings with such a person.

This is because neither of you know much about the other person. You nor the other know what you can offer or what the other person wishes to bring into the potential professional relationship.

This is a true story: following a friend's well-intended advice, I phoned a reputable gallery owner with the aim of having a meeting with him. I wanted to show him some of my tapestries. When he answered the phone, I introduced myself explaining to him that I had made a tapestry themed from one of the Group of Seven (Canadian landscape artists). I had a chance to continue, I was interrupted by the gallery owner who proceeded to lecture me on the history of the Group of Seven, in that, *"they were oil painters and they never made any tapestries."* This followed with another lecture of a crash-course in **Canadian art history, and** *"please do not call me again"*.

Had I tried to correct him, it would had been beyond the scope of my initial purpose of the phone call. How often such misunderstandings happen would not be believed by you or me alone.

Having said that, all kinds of strategies can be played out of how to approach major gallery owners, curators of fibre museums, agents and other players who are in a unique position to channel your career success.

The percentage is not in your favour if you merely try to "Hi my name is Constantine and I'm a tapessier specializing in pictorial tapestries".

While you may think that this is a good enough reason for you to attempt to meet persons in some kind of beneficial symbiotic social status, it will not apply to them. Here are some of the more important reasons that may entice someone to meet/engage with you: a) because they share with you a common professional interest. b) you know a mutual person of influence c) that you have something that these people **need**, and therefore 'there-is-something-for them', by way of interaction with you.

So, when you are about to embark on your journey into the world of influence, ensure that the meeting with influential people **it more about them and less about you.**

Now, let us assume for a moment that I have a good reason to meet a reputable gallery owner; do I go before such a person and say "Hi my name is Constantine, and Mr. Intermediary asked me to call you and talk to you". No I would not do so unless Mr. Intermediary has already talked to this person, knows of my background in the art of tapestries, and so on.

The best way to meet someone of social status is by personal introduction arranged by an intermediary who is in good standing; one who knows you and the gallery owner. This is a more effective way than introducing yourself. The intermediary who introduces you functions as an instant character reference, a concrete indication that the meeting has a solid base for the potential to become actual or, alternatively, it's worthwhile for it to take place.

Even with an introduction, there is no guarantee that would result in something tangible. It happens when the intermediary 'over helps' you by promising more tapestries than you have or more talent than you are able to exhibit or is making commitments on your behalf that you cannot meet.

More than often, the majority of successful networkings are initiated between fibre artists who already know each other. Very few outstanding tapessiers would be willing to introduce a total stranger, and this is why you should network with other *of your calibre* in the fibre arts.

Making 'cold-calling' or 'cold e-mailing' rarely works unless you have something out of the ordinary, unbelievable, and astonishing to risk a cold-call about.

Visit as many fibre art expositions as you can spare the time and make casual conversations with other fibre artists or persons of interest. However, in such brief encounters people tend to forget one another unless they have something from the other person that causes them to remember their encounter with you. Bring with you your business cards (your miniature post cards) and pass them on in any vital opportunity. I've found that a picture of a quality tapestry printed as a business card, with all pertinent information at the back of the card, creates an ideal opening for a brief conversation. The picture of your tapestry will be the connecting medium between two or more people.

If something good happens, out of such a casual conversations, that's great; if not, wait until next time Remember, networking is just one of many ways of meeting others. In the case of networking, let the experience be the reward in and of itself.

The basic rule of networking is to maintain the minimum, and not to over-network, unless you get the feeling that the person you're networking with wants to be networked on. Only when the conversation appears serious, then and only then, you begin to network, otherwise you'll risk appearing as a home carpet salesman trying too hard to sell. In the manner of your actions, you will attract others and find yourself on a common ground immersed in circumstances where everyone's acting similarly.

When you are networking, be as casual as you can be without making the other person fall asleep; and do not get over-analytical about methodology of networking. But you must have a clear notion about who attends fibre expositions (the playground of networking) and ask yourself whether you are prepared to work with these people; gallery owners, curators of fibre museums and agents, all are essential parts of the fibre artist's environment. Most sell fibre art on consignment for a living.

Are you prepared to meet these people for the purpose of placing your tapestries on consignment? Remember, these are the professionals who know how to spread the word for they invest the time, effort, promotional skills, and have the overhead and exhibition space necessary to assist you to expand the list of your clients, and attain critical recognition within the fibre arts community. Sure you can network as much as you like, but at the same time, having a trustworthy agent or gallery owner with an established record, can advance your career a lot.

Whatever road you choose to expand your networking and your career as a tapessier, do not have preconceived ideas. Do not do it alone, do not be an island, for it will be hard to be all things necessary: getting your name out, getting the attention of the fibre art community and, at the same time, creating fine in-laid pictorial tapestries. Networking allows you to stand alone, a valid compromise, if you are reluctant to accept an agent (that you do not know), a gallery owner whom you do not trust, or a fibre art curator that makes you feel as a second-class citizen.

As you go along with your career as a fine tapessier, take your time and evaluate the results of your networking, and avoid those who have no professional value trying a better arrangement somewhere else. This way, you get a gradual feel of how to go about with the fibre art business of your studio.

Finally, do whatever it takes not to become a classic case of the Master Tapessier whose Inlaid Pictorial Tapestries get recognition they deserve, only after they are dead!!

GENERAL OBSERVATIONS OF THE DO AND DON'TS

WHAT TO AVOID:

- Do not act important, especially at times when you have a client that does not know much about inlaid tapestries, or in an open-to-the-public studio show.
- Do not make yourself inaccessible; that will make potential clients uncomfortable to approach you.
- Do not behave like you are the last egg in the picnic basket. By having a superior attitude and/or not acknowledging the presence of your visitors is a sure way of eliminating them.
- Do not pay exclusive attention to visitors who are familiar to you, while ignoring all others.
- Do not appear overly busy (busy bee?) that you do not have time to talk with your visitors.
- Do not act impatient, as if someone who is more important is waiting for you, and give short and abrupt answers to visitor's questions about your inlaid tapestries.
- Do not try to convince your clients, who prefer a lower priced tapestry, to purchase another more expensive one.
- Display modestly priced tapestries as prominently as those that are more expensive, for you do not want your clients to think that those are left overs.
- Do not raise your prices for the 'open-house', rather set a lower percentage which is a good way to attract clients and sell out.
- Set your studio with a gallery setting, and do not 'overload' your space with every tapestry you ever made. Choose a price level that will attract also those with a lower budget.
- Do not be a 'downer' complaining about the public's lack of understanding of your fibre artwork.
- Do not hide modesty priced tapestries and only present the most expensive ones.

- Do not act offended when a client asks for a discount off the asking price, and do not act unhappy when you accept an offer of a lower price.
- Do not give the impression to your clients that you are the best and every other tapessier is of a lower 'cast'.
- Do not try to impress your visitors by using tapessier's jargon that is unintelligible and gibberish (to them).
- Particularly important is to not ask your clients if they understand what you are saying when you explain something about your tapestry.
- Do not act offended when your visitors misinterpret your inlaid pictorial tapestries technique for print-on-textile.
- Do not show to your clients disrespect for other tapessier's artwork and elevate yours.
- Do not overindulge in booze and drugs at your 'open studio' gallery events or public fibre expositions.
- Keep your gallery's walking space clear, and do not have tapestries sit on the floor and/or lean against the wall; it appears as if they are waiting to be hung for the opening of your gallery show.
- Finally, do not just talk to visitors that you think they are more likely to buy a tapestry.

IS CONSIGNMENT FOR YOU?

Let's assume the following; that you are working out of your home and that you are not participating in the Internet or have an open-to-the-public studio. Your home is a great location, in so far as, you do not have to travel, and though your space may be somewhat restricted it is presumably comfortable. In other words, your overhead operating cost is low. Your market outlet may also be limited to consignment as a way to reach potential customers. Is consignment for you?

As is the case in most diversified galleries, agents and fibre museums receiving tapestries on consignment is a normal method of doing business.

In turn, you as a tapessier, must trust the gallery owner, your agent and the museum to take care of your valuable fibre art, make the sales in a pre-agreed price and get paid on time.

So why then do so many fibre artists have so many consignment problems with galleries, agents, and museums? Some tapessiers have problems with collecting their money, some have their tapestries 'lost' or stolen or damaged, and some were told that their tapestries were not sold, when in fact, the opposite was true. However, viewing all diversified galleries, agents and museums as evil, is detrimental to your sales. Simply put, do not let a few dishonest dealers distort your beliefs and attitude about dealers in general.

Choosing the right kind of dealer, is a rough-science to say the least. Some general guidelines, however, may help you to make a better choice:

- Does the dealer show a vivid respect to you as an fibre artist? If not, just walk away!

- If you feel uncomfortable (in any way or form) with the dealer, simply walk out and avoid future problems!

- Initially, base your decision on an instinctual gut level; chances are that you made an accurate judgement!

- Then, pay attention to your instinctual warning signs, like minor difference of opinion, style of dealer's negotiations. These factors must not be ambiguous or uncomfortable to you!

PRICING YOUR TAPESTRIES

Before we go into details about pricing your tapestry, allow me to say this to you; you must treat yourself and your fibre artwork with the respect you both deserve. As all fine tapessiers must, treat your fibre art as art, (as serious as anyone takes their chosen profession or calling). As an inlaid tapessier, you must accept and promote a social obligation to install that notion into other tapessiers whether you are a member of a guild or not. At the same time, you must be modest, don't be a snob! Don't fill yourself with false self-esteem, and with a notion of self-importance.

If other tapessiers do not create as fine a fibre artwork as you, snobiness will only create divisions among members of the tapessier community. Help those with less talent to improve theirs, which in turn would educate the public to distinguish a fine tapestry from a lesser one. Encourage other weavers to try this 'new' exciting form of in-laid tapestry with tips and brief techniques – freely given.

Demonstrate to weavers and tapessiers that transforming a complex idea into a technical sound and thought provoking fibre artwork, is a talent that takes time, focus and discipline to acquire, that they too can develop and possess. Above all, emphasize to tapessiers not to treat their in-laid Pictorial Tapestry as a 'trinket' to be sold into the lesser markets. And, there you have it; my purest vision. I am speaking to you from experience! I once took a fine tapestry to a "Gift and Craft" shop to see if my kind of fibre artwork could possibly be sold in such places. I sat and watched for a few hours as people had come and gone passing in front of my tapestry on the wall, and hardly anyone paid more than a passing glance at my tapestry. I returned the next day; to my horror, someone from the staff pinned a small piece of paper on it directing people to the public washrooms!! I swear this is God's truth. The same tapestry was sold by a fine diversified gallery for $2,400 about 2 months later.

Therefore, pricing your in-laid Pictorial Tapestry must be based on certain criteria:

- In what kind of establishment are you planning to offer your tapestry?

- Can you divide those establishments into 3 categories? 1) average, 2) above average, 3) exclusive. These criteria should be based on your own evalution of the kind of establishments located in your market area. For example the 3rd category would be galleries located in Lake Louise Hotel, 2nd in any diversified gallery located in an artist district of a metropolitan city (Toronto, New York), and 1st fibre galleries and museums of standing.

- Classification of inlaid tapesties must be based on the above criteria: 1st) less intricate, 2nd) more intricate, 3rd) very intricate.

- Within these classifications there should also be included the actual size tapestry; and this is determined by the market's demand.

- Based on the above criteria, figure out how much your tapestry is worth and where to sell it and 'how' to offer it for sale.

Let's talk about intricate in-laid Pictorial Tapestry. For obvious reasons, the more intricate the tapestry is the higher the asking price should be. This is true, whether you are a well-known tapessier artist or not. Let's side-track for a moment.

Let's assume that you are a novice tapessier, with little or no experience. However skillful as a tapessier you may be, there is little point in inlaying just an intricate pictorial tapestry. You see, apart from your talent and studies in the art of inlaid tapestry, what someone is willing to pay for it would depend on whether you are recognized and associated with this kind of intricate fibre artwork. To arrive at the point of wide spread recognition, you must appeal to serious collectors who are willing to pay a given price to own one or more of your tapestries.

Let's assume that you are exhibiting a Pictorial Tapestry with an identical theme in three fibre art galleries, each rated with the 1, 2, and 3 categories given in the previous example. The price of your tapestry will very much depend on who is visiting these galleries, and the category of the establishment. In the 1st gallery category the visitors tend to be real estate and travel salesmen who may be willing to pay a few hundred dollars for a fibre work. In the 2nd category, upcoming junior executives will look for something to go with the general décor of their condo; in this case the asking price may go up a bit. In the number 3 category of tapestry (and gallery), you may price your Pictorial Tapestry based on the intricacy of your tapestry, and the type of establishment in which you are offering your Pictorial Tapestry.

How do you price your tapestry? You meet the category criteria outlined above!

From a fibre art point of view, the less intricate the Pictorial Tapestry is, the lower the asking price. In the case of the three categories of diversified fibre art galleries, your tapestry's intricacy should reflect the same degrees of comparison.

Think about this a moment: what would happen if you place in a 3rd category gallery, all three categories of tapestry intricacy? This would mean that you are offering collectors a choice of pictorial tapestries: a simple (few hundred dollars), a complex (up the price a bit), and an intricate (a significant increase). The reverse will cause a failure, for exhibiting in a 1st category gallery a 3rd category tapestry would not produce desired results.

How many categories of tapestries that you create will very much depend on your sales. Therefore, you must price your tapestries reasonably. Create what sell, and sell in establishments where fibre artworks sell often.

HOW TO ADD VALUE TO YOUR TAPESTRY

An in-laid Pictorial Tapestry is an attractive fibre artwork that can be made more attractive in order to add value to it. The aim is to sell it. That is as simple as that and no more complicated.

SYMBOLIC SIGNATURE

The most important thing you can do is to sign your Pictorial Tapestry, without exception. Embedded within the tapestry's body or at the bottom heading (plain weave), **a Symbolic Signature** of your own creation would be consistent with that of the Great Masters of Tapestries,

Regardless if you, as a tapessier, longing for fame or not you must not design your pictorial tapestries without a Symbolic Signature that identifies who is the artist tapessier. You see, at this point in time no one knows you by your tapestries nor your tapestries by their excellence. But, one day, as you become well known you must tell your community, your neighbourhood, your city, your state or province, your country and the rest of the world who you are!

A Symbolic Signature must be simple, appropriate in composition, legible, and should be executed in a darker/lighter wool colour, but in a simple tone. It should be placed in the right bottom corner of your tapestry's main body or in the heading. In other words, it must be inlaid or weaved and form an integral part of the artwork. Choose your Symbolic Signature carefully, and do not change your style, for it will cause confusion between your current Pictorial Tapestry and the one of the past. Study over the Symbolic Signatures of the Great Masters of Tapestries you are about to create; it is worth while! !

SHORT TITLE

As with the Symbolic Signature, a **Title** should be simple and appropriate in its composition and legibility. You could weave in border linen or inlaided in the main tapestry's body. If, on the other hand, you are planning to frame your tapestry, you may wish to place a small brass plate in the right bottom corner of the frame. An electric engraver you could engrave the title, date and name.

DATE IT

Most collectors would prefer knowing when the Pictorial Tapestry was made. **Symbolic Signature**, **Title** and **Date** would demonstrate to the collector the value of your fibre art. Most collectors like to show off their latest acquisitions of pictorial tapestries. When viewers ask collectors about your creation, if there is no Symbolic Signature, Title and Date, there is no confirmed identity of the fibre art made by you.

The more your in-laid tapestries are identified with you, as the tapessier artist, the more your name becomes known -- and the collectors like to brag to other collectors about knowing you personally.

Case in point: this happened in Ontario, Canada. One day I went to a friend's house looking for a hand tool. When I realized that his house was full of people, I was tempted to turn around and leave. My friend saw me in time and invited me to stay. He explained to me that I was there opportunely at the right time to listen to his guests talking about my friend's latest acquisition of six of my tapestries hanging high on his home's walls. He briefly introduced me to all and I was left alone.

They were all involved in a lively discussion about the inlaid pictorial tapestries my friend had purchased; whether the tapestries were actual paintings or, if they were printed on fabric, Since, most of his visitors had not seen an inlaid pictorial tapestry, they could not comprehend that it was possible to 'hand-weave' a tapestry with such fine details. My friend found such discussion amusing and wanted me to be present to hear them talking about my creations.

I don't know whether it was my construction clothes or my general appearance, like I said before, but I was left alone, until, that is, my friend Jim introduced me once again by stating "and this is the artist of my tapestries."

Following a brief explanation of how-to-inlay-a-tapestry I had requests for a commissioned work from several people 'who meet the artist' in person. See my point?

A few more effortless value enhancers: take a picture of yourself holding your tapestry, shoot a video of yourself inlaying your tapestry, give a CD to your client, and explain it, in a handwritten style (on good quality paper) also giving it to your client. If your handwriting is as bad as mine, have someone do it for you. Then, keep a record of all your Inlaid Pictorial Tapestries. One day you'll be glad you did!

English and Metric Conversion Tables.

Metric to English Measurements.

To convert from:	To:	Multiply the metric unit by:
Length		
Meters	yards	1.093
Meters	feet	3.280
Meters	inches	39.370
Centimeters	inches	.394
Millimeters	inches	.039
Area and Volume		
Square meters	square yards	1.196
Square meters	square feet	10.764
Square centimeters	square inches	.155
Cubic centimeters	cubic inches	.061
Liquid Measure		
Litres	cubic inches	61.020
Litres	cubic feet	.035
Litres	U.S. gallons*	.264
Litres	U.S. quarts*	1.057
Weight and Mass		
Kilograms	pounds	2.205
Grams	ounces	.035
Grams	grains	15.430
Grams per meter	ounces per yard	.032
Grams per square meter	ounces per square yard	.030

English Measurements to Metric

To convert from:	To:	Multiply the English unit by:
Length		
Yards	meters	.914
Feet	meters	.305
Inches	meters	.025
Inches	centimeters	2.540
Inches	millimeters	25.400
Area and Volume		
Square yards	square meters	.836
Square feet	square meters	.093
Square inches	square centimeters	6.451
Cubic inches	cubic centimeters	16.387
Liquid measure		
Cubic inches	litres	.016
Cubic feet	litres	28.339
U.S. gallons*	litres	3.785
U.S. quarts*	litres	.946
Weight and Mass		
Pounds	kilograms	.453
Ounces	grams	28.349
Grains	grams	.065
Ounces per yard	grams per meter	31.250
Ounces per square yard	grams per square meter	33.333

* The British imperial gallon equals approximately 1.2 U.S. gallons or 4.54 litres. Similarly, the British imperial quart is 1.2 U.S., and so on.

CANADIAN AND AMERICAN HANDWEAVER'S ASSOCIATIONS

HANDWEAVERS GUILD OF AMERICA
3327 Duluth Street 201
Duluth, GA 30096
Ph: (770) 495-7702
Fx: (770) 495-7706
E-mail: weavespindye@compuserve.com

GUILD OF CANADIAN WEAVERS
714 Hazell Road
Kelowna, BC V1W IR3
Web: www.the-gcw.org

ALBERTA CRAFT COUNCIL
10186-106 Street
Edmonton, AB T5N 1H4
Ph: (780) 488-6611
Fx: (780) 488-8855
Toll Free: 1-800-362-7238
E-mail: acc@albertacraft.ab.ca

LETHBRIDGE HANDCRAFT GUILD
Bowman Art Centre
811 - 5th Avenue
South Lethbridge, AB T1J 0V2
Ph: (403) 328-7488
Affiliation: Handweavers, Spinners and Dyers of Alberta

ONTARIO CRAFT COUNCIL
Designers Walk # 300, 170 Bedford Road
Toronto, Ontario M5R 2K9
Ph: (416) 925-4222
Fx: (416) 925-4223
E-mail: nmorrison@craft.on.ca
Web: www.craft.on.ca

NEW BRUNSWICK CRAFT COUNCIL
P.O. Box 1231
Fredericton, NB E3B 5C8
Ph: (506) 450-8989
Fx: (506) 457-6010
E-mail: nbcrafts@nb.aibn.ccrn

NOVA SCOTIA DESIGNER CRAFT COUNCIL
1113 Marginal Road
Halifax, NS B3H 4P7
Ph: (902) 423-3837
Fx: (902) 422-0881
E-mail: office@nsdcc.ns.ca
Web: www.nsdcc.ns.ca

PRINCE EDWARD ISLAND CRAFT COUNCIL
156 Richmond Street
Charlottetown, PE C1A 1H9
Ph: (902) 892-5152
Fx: (902) 628-8740
E-mail: info@peicraftscounsil.com

SASKATCHEWAN CRAFT COUNCIL
813 Broadway Avenue
Saskatoon, SK S7N 1B5
Ph: (306) 653-3616
Fx: (306) 244-2711
E-mail: saskcraftcounsil@shaw.ca
Web: www.saskcraftcounsil.org

AMERICAN TAPESTRY BIENNIAL 6
36840 Detroit Road
Avon, Ohio 44011
Web: www.americantapestryalliance.org

WEAVE A REAL PEASE
3102 Classen Boulevard, PMB 249
Oklahoma City, OK 73118
Web: w3.thegroup.net/janis/warp.html

THE WEAVERS FRIED AND THE LOOM MANUAL LIBRARY
5672 North Shore Drive
Duluth, MN 55804
Web: www.weaversfriend.ccm

ASSOCIATION OF SOUTHERN CALIFORNIA HANDWEAVERS
Ph: (526) 420-7844
E-mail: phusby@pcclubnet.com

AMERICAN CRAFT COUNCIL
72 Spring Street, 6th Floor
New York, NY 10012-4019
Ph: (212) 274-0630
Fx: (212) 274-0650
E-mail: counsil@craftcounsil.org
Web: www.craftcounsil.org

PARKLAND HANDWEAVERS & SPINNERS ASSOCIATION
211, 4638 Ross Street
Red Deer, AB T4N 6B3

HALIBURTON HIGHLANDS GUILD OF FINE ARTS
P.O. Box 912
Haliburton, ON K0M 1S0
Ph: (705) 457-2330
Fx: (705) 457-2338
E-mail: hhgfa.railsend@on.aibn.com
Web: www.auriga.on.ca/hal/rails.html

MANITOBA CRAFT COUNCIL
237 McDermond Avenue
Winnipeg, MB R3B 0S4
Ph: (204) 487-6114
Fx: (204) 487-6115
E-mail: info@craftspace.org
Web: www.craftspace.org

HERITAGE WEAVERS AND SPINNERS GUILD
R.R.# 1
Limehouse, ON L0P 1H0
Ph. (905) 877-9404
E-mail: m.doole@3web.net

AMERICAN TAPESTRY ALLIANCE
328 Leigton Street
Cambia, CA 93428
Ph: (805) 927-1976
Fx: (805) 927-1946
E-mail: judysarts@thegrid.net

CONFERENCE OF NORTHERN CALIFORNIA HANDWEAVERS
www.cnch.org

AMERICAN ARTS AND CRAFTS ALLIANCE
425 Riverside Drive, Apt. 15
New York, NY 10025
Ph: (212) 866-2239

EDMONTON WEAVERS GUILD
Prince of Wales Armouries
Box 4, 10440 - 108 Avenue
Edmonton, AB T5H 3Z9
E-mail: ehett@planet.eon.net
Web: www.freenet.edmonton.ab.ca/weavers

MEDICINE HAT FIBRE ARTS SOCIETY
c/o Cultural Centre
299 College Drive South East
Medicine Hat, AB T1A 3Y6
Ph: (403) 529-1174

MUSKOKA ARTS & CRAFT Inc
P.O. Box 376
Bracebridge, ON P1L 1T7
Web: www.muskokaartsandcrafts.com

OTTAWA VALLEY WEAVERS AND SPINNERS GUILD
The Centre, Heartwood House
153 Chapel Street
Ottawa, ON K1N 1H5
Web: www.ovwsg.com

SUDBURY WEAVERS AND SPINNERS GUILD
Web: www.bigfoot.com/~sudburyweavers

CAMBRIDGE WEAVERS AND SPINNERS GUILD
Ph: (519) 647-2233
E-mail: troyspr@sentex.net

KINGSTON HANDLOOM WEAVERS AND SPINNERS
Web: www.khws.ca

CANADIAN GUILD OF CRAFTS
1460, rue Sherbrook ouest
Montreal, QC H3G 1K4
Ph: (514) 849-6091
Fx: (403) 291-0675
Toll Free: 1-866-477-6091
E-mail: info@canadianguild.com
Web: www.canadianguild.com

THE SARNIA HANDWEAVERS AND SPINNERS GUILD
Web: www.sarnia.com/groups/weave-spin

CRAFT COUNSIL OF NEWFOUNDLAND & LABRADOR
Devon House
59 Duckworth Street
St. John's, NL A1C 1E6
Ph: (709) 753-2749
Fx: (709) 753-2766
E-mail: info@craftcounsil.nf.ca
Web: www.craftcounsil.nf.ca

CRAFT ASSOCIATION OF BRITISH COLUMBIA
Granville Island, 1386 Cartwright Street
Vancouver, BC V6H 3R8
Ph: (604) 687-6511
Fx: (604) 687-6711
Toll Free: 1-888-687-6511
E-mail: cabc@telus.net
Web: www.cabc.net

MISSISSIPPI VALLEY TEXTILE MUSEUM
3 Rosamund Street
East Almonte, ON K0A1A0
Ph: (613) 256-3754
E-mail: textile@magma.ca
Web: www.textilemuseum.mississippimills.com

MID-ATLANTIC FIBER ASSOCIATION
Web: www.mafafiber.org

MID-WEST WEAVERS ASSOCIATION
Web: http://home.fuse.net/weavers/

COMPLEX WEAVERS
1615 Avenue North
Seattle, WA 98109
Web: www.complex-weavers.org

CANADIAN CRAFT AND HOBBY ASSOCIATION
#24, 1410-40 Avenue North East
Calgary, AB T2E 6L1
Ph: (403) 291-0559
Fx: (403) 291-0675
Toll Free: 1-888-991-0559

FOLK ARTS COUNCIL DF WINNIPEG
183 Kennedy Street, 2nd Floor
Winnipeg, MB R3C 1S6
Ph: (204) 982-6210
Fx: (204) 943-1956
Toll Free: 1-800-665-0234
E-mail: folkarts@folkorama.ca
Web: www.folkorama.ca

QUALICUM WEAVERS AND SPINNERS
831 Glenhale Crescent
Parkville, BC V9P 1Z8
Ph: (250) 954-1205

THE CORVALUS HANDWEAVERS AND SPINNERS GUILD
Web: www.artcentric.org

TEXTILE MUSEUM OF CANADA
55 Centre Avenue
Toronto, ON M5G 2H5
Ph: (416) 599-2239
Fx: (416) 599-2911
E-mail: info@textilemseum.ca
Web: www.textilemuseum.ca

CANADIAN CO-OPERATIVE WOOL GROWERS

http://www.wool.ca

BRITISH COLUMBIA

Dave Cadsand	(604) 395-4242
Ian Dalziel	1-866-965-9665
Joybilee Farm	(Toll free)
Gail Henderson	(604) 782-1431
Heinz Krauskopf	(250) 786-0225
Christy Robley	(250) 537-7440

ALBERTA

CCWG	(403) 327-3760
Dan Cadsand (Jr.)	(403) 843-6253
Danny Cahoon	(403) 653-2627
Edwin Cahoon	(403) 653-2266
Dave Carlson	(403) 553-4268
Ian Dalziel	1-866-965-9665
Ed Dingreville	(403) 628-2235
Henk Dorenbos	(780) 305-4193
John Grab	(403) 843-3660
Bryce Gore	(403) 932-2866
John Head	(780) 672-3538
Lorne Knodel	(403) 527-9782
Heinz Krauskopf	(250) 786-0225
Brian McLeod	(780) 696-3605
Joe Milne	(780) 892-2826
Duane O'Brien	(780) 672-6514

SASKATCHEWAN

Clifford Metheral	(306) 528-2113
Kendall Smith	(306) 825-3770
Lorrie Reed	(306) 378-4010
Francis Ecker	(306) 837-4762
Lovern Struck	(306) 367-4278
Buddy Wilmink	(306) 778-9134
Wayne Garnett	(306) 883-2928

MANITOBA

Howard Alexander	(204) 467-9399
Herb Benson	(204) 835-2556
Brian Greaves	(204) 567-3509
Brian Harper	(204) 725-2515
Roy Leitch	(204) 727-5021
Wayne Petre	(204) 435-2437
Eric Thornhill	(204) 257-7456

GLOSSARY
FIBRE STUDIO

BACK BEAM. The fixed upper beam at the back of the loom directly above the warp at even tension through its smooth surface.

BEAMING. To roll the warp onto the warp beam under tension.

BEATER. The movable framework that holds the reed. Pulling it forward pushes the weft into place. The beater can be base-mounted in jack looms or swing freely on counter-marche-type looms.

BOBBIN. Thread that is wound around this quill before it is inserted into the shuttle.

BREAST OR FRONT BEAM. The fixed upper beam at front of loom over which the tapestry passes to the fabric beam below.

CASTLE. The central main framework of the loom that supports the harness.

CHAIN. A series of continuous thread loops made in the warp to temporarily shorten its length, for easy handling and transporting to the loom preventing its tangling.

CHAIN-SPACER. A series of continuous thread loops made around the warp ends. Used mainly on frame looms before in-laid wool begins. It keeps warp threads evenly spaced.

CLOTH OR FABRIC BEAM. The rotating lower front beam of the loom. The finished tapestry is rolled as it is in-laid.

CROSS. Formed as the figure eight made as warp ends cross in alternate succession around pegs on a reel or warping board. It too prevents tangles.

DENT. The space between two bars in a reed. Reeds are made in various sizes based on the number of dents per inch. An 8-dent reed has 8 dents per inch.

DRAWN-IN. The pulling inwards of the selvedges from the intended weight during the passing of weft.

DRESSING THE LOOM. Another term for preparing the loom for warping.

END. An individual length or strand warp.

FELL OR HEADING. The narrow edge of fabric woven to the front and end of the tapestry. It provides a strong support to withstand stretching and load.

ENDS PER INCH. Indicates how many warp ends are in one inch.

FIBRES. Are the natural or synthetic filaments which when spun together form a thread or yarn. Fibre can be the raw material whose origins may come from animal, vegetable or mineral.

FILLER. Unlike the normal definition associated with yarn-weft, here the term refers to wool that is in-laid using weft for interlocking it.

HARNESS. Two or more frames in the centre of the loom and between which the heddles are hung.

HEADING. A narrow strip of fabric woven at the beginning and at the end of the in-laid tapestry that provides support and strength.

HEDDLE. A flat metal, wire or string with a loop or eye in its centre that is hung between the harness. It holds the warp ends in a fixed position.

JACK LOOM. A loom with a rising shed; that is, a number of warp threads lifted from the horizontal position to make a shed. See also rising shed.

LAMS OR LAMMS. Horizontal bars or levers that are located between the harnesses and treadles (and attached to both on a floor loom.

LEASE. See cross.

LEASE STICKS OR RODS. Flat, thin, smooth and sometimes round sticks inserted into the warp on either side of the cross in warping to hold the cross in place.

LEVERS. The bars on table loom which raise the harness when pressed.

LOOM WASTE. This is the part of the warp on the loom that is not weaved and, therefore, is wasted at the front and back of the tapestry.

LOOM. A frame for holding the warp threads under tension so the weaving can be processed.

MORDANTS. See glossary on Dyeing.

PLAIN WEAVE. The most basic weave that is required for the in-laid tapestry. It is woven by raising every even weave warp thread over every odd numbered weft shot and every odd numbered thread over every even shot.

PICK. A single pass of weft thread through the shed, also called shot.

QUILL. A paper tube onto which the weft thread is wound for insertion in the shuttle.

RATCHED. A wheel with notches or teeth, holding the ends of warp and cloth beams to secure proper tension and to prevent both from unrolling.

REED. A metal frame that fits into the beater to space warp threads according to plan. Also to beat the weft in weaving.

REED HOOK. A hand held device with a hook at one end, used to pull the warp ends through the heddle eyes and reed slits or dents.

RISING SHED. A shed opening made by the raising of even or odd numbered warp threads.

ROVING. A rope-like form of wool ready to be in-laid.

ROW. A single shot of weft.

SELVEDGE. A warpwise edge of the tapestry that doesn't unravel.

SETT. The number of warp threads per inch.

SHED. The V-shaped opening formed by the lowering or raising of warp ends. Through the shed passes the shuttle carrying the weft thread.

SHOT. See pick.

SLEY. Threading the warp through the dents of the reed.

SLEY HOOK. See reed hook.

TABBY. See plain weave.

TENSION. The degree of tightness to which the warp is stretched on the loom.

TENSION STICK. A thin flat stick used in a frame loom inserted into the warp to adjust the tension.

THRUMS. See loom waste.

TIE-UP. Reference to the method by which the treadles are secured to the lamms of the loom.

TREADLES. The foot pedals that are attached to the lamms on floor looms and raise or lower them.

WARP. The threads that are running lengthwise in the loom.

WARPING. Measuring the warp and/or winding and securing the warp to both the back and front beams, and includes sleying the reed and the heddles.

WARP BEAM. The beam at the back of the loom onto which the warp is rolled.

WARP PLAN. See drawing-in.

WARPING BOARD. A frame revolving wheel around which the warp is measured and wound.

WEFT. The yarn that is interwoven with the warp ends.

GLOSSARY
FOR THE DYER'S STUDIO

ACETIC ACID (VINEGAR). It is used to increase the acid level in both dye and vat bath.

ALKALI (OR BASE). Is the opposite to acid in the pH scale.

ALUM. A mordant frequently used with adherent dyes. Also known as potassium aluminum sulfate.

ANIMAL FIBRE. Material which includes sheep wool, llama, mohair, alpaca, angora, etc., that are used for spinning yarn and for in-laid wool.

AUXILLIARIES. Are acids for dyes in the dyeing process. Alum, citric acid and cream of tartar are some of the most widely used substances. The use of auxiliaries in themselves do not impact colour.

CELLULOSE FIBRES. Are fibres derived from plants such as cotton and hemp.

CITRIC ACID. It is used to increase acid levels in both dye and vat baths.

CHEMICAL REDUCTION. This method uses a reducing agent that affects the oxygen and alkali level in the dyeing process.

CHROMA. The term refers to the intensity or the de-saturation of colour. Intensity of colour can be achieved by adding black. Desaturation of colour will have more grey in it.

COMPLIMENTARY COLOURS. Are these located opposite to each other on the colour wheel.

CREAM OF TARTAR. This is used when mordating wool fibres in order to improve smoothness and brightness in certain colours.

DEPTH OF SHADE. It refers to the ratio of the lightness or darkness of a colour.

DYE STOCK SOLUTION. A pre-made solution of dye/water ratio that is made for measuring the amount of dye needed, and also for convenience. It saves time and work by avoiding making small quantities of dye solution for each dye needed.

FASTNESS. The term refers to the longevity of a dye colour. In the case of the in-laid wool tapestry that will be hanging on the wall and exposed to bright light; a dye will be needed that has an excellent light fastness.

FELTING. A condition that affects wool fibre when moisture, heat, agitation and rapid drop in temperature causes the matting of the fibre.

HAZARDOUS MORDANT. These are CHROME (potassium dichromate), COPPER (cooper sulfate), and TIN (stannous chlorite). There are hazardous to both humans and the environment. Avoid using them.

HUE. It is the main characteristic that separates one colour from another.

IMMERSION DYEING. A dye bath with a regulated water/dye whose volume permits the immersion of wool.

INSOLUBLE. Vat dyes (both natural and synthetic) that are not water-soluble. These require a special process to make the dye fixate to the wool. Synthetic vat dyes can only be used after they are converted by chemical reduction. See natural fermentation.

LEVEL DYEING. A uniformed distribution of dyeing wool fibre.

LEVELING AGENT. A substance used to create a uniformed level of dyeing.

LIGHTFASTNESS. See fastness.

LYE. A substance that raises the pH level of alkali in both bath and vat dyes. Note: remember to always add lye to water, not the other way around.

MORDANT. Aide substance that facilitates and improves the fastness of natural dyes. It is combined with dye and fibre.

NATURAL DYES. These are the **adherents** that require a mordant to aid a dye and improve the colour's fastness.

Direct dyes combine with the fibre and do not require mordant or special handling.

NATURAL FERMENTATION. It is done by adding organic material (i.e. vegetable peelings) and allowed to decompose and ferment in order to reduce the oxygen in the solution.

SAFE MORDANTS. Alum (potassium aluminum sulfate), and iron (ferrous sulfate) also know as copperas and green vitriol.

SCOURING. The term refers to washing wool, after removing dirt, particles, de-selecting size and other contaminants that may prevent the proper dyeing of wool.

SECONDARY COLOURS. These are the results of mixing pairs of primary colours: Red & Yellow = Orange, Red & Blue = Purple, and Blue & Yellow = Green.

SIMULTANEOUS MORDANT. Refers to adding the mordant to the dye pot at the same time with the dye.

PH. Method to determine the acidity or the alkalinity of a solution. A pH scale ranges from 0 to 14 with 7 being a neutral solution. Acidity of solution increases downwards from 7 to 0; alkalinity increases from 7 to 14. A normal level should range between pH 5 and 12.

POSTMORDATING. This is done right after the dye process, as long as, the wool was not premordated.

PREMORDATING. It refers to use of mordant before the dye process takes place.

PRIMARY COLOURS. Red, Blue, and Yellow. Those are the basic colours in the colour wheel.

TERTIARY COLOURS. These are the results of mixing a primary colour with a secondary colour that is attached to it onto the colour wheel. Thus, Red-Orange, Yellow-Green, Yellow-Orange, Blue-Green, Blue-Purple, and Red-Purple are tertiary colours.

VALUE. The term refers to the degree of lightness or darkness of a colour. When compared to light or dark shade, pink is a 'light' red and burgundy is a 'dark' value of red.

VAT DYES. See insoluble.

INDEX

FIBRE ARTIST STUDIO

BACK BEAM 102
BEATER 86, 102 to 105
BOBBIN 88, 92
BREAST OR FRONT BEAM 104
CASTLE 102
CHAIN 99 to 102
CLOTH OR FABRIC BEAM 95, 102, 104 to 106
CROSS 97, 98, 99, 102
DENT 103, 104
DRAWN-IN 94, 102
DRESSING THE LOOM 104
END 84, 86 TO 90, 92, 94, 95, 97, 99, 103, 106
FELL OR HEADING 94, 95, 106
ENDS PER INCH 94
FIBRES (see protein fibre)
FILLER (see in-laid wool)
HARNESS 85, 86, 102, 103, 105, 106
HEADING 94, 95, 96, 97, 106
HEDDLE 86, 88, 89, 90, 91, 95, 96, 102, 103, 104
JACK LOOM 84, 85
LAMS OR LAMMS 105
LEASE (see cross)
LEASE STICKS OR RODS 102
LEVERS 86
LOOM WASTE 94, 95

LOOM 84 to 88, 90 to 95, 108
MORDANTS (see dyeing)
PLAIN WEAVE 94, 96, 106
PICK (see weft)
REED 86, 94, 95, 102 to 105
REED HOOK 103
RISING SHED 84 to 88, 91, 106
ROW 96, 97, 106
SETT 86, 87, 88, 94, 103
SHED 86, 87, 88, 91, 106
SHOT (see pick)
SLEY HOOK (see reed hook)
TABBY (see plain weave)
TENSION 86, 87, 94, 95, 98, 102, 104, 105
TENSION STICK 86, 87, 90
TREADLES 86
WARP 86 to 89, 91 to 103
WARPING (see warp)
WARP BEAM 102, 104, 105
WARPING BOARD 97, 99
WEFT 84, 86, 87, 92 to 106

I N D E X

DYER'S STUDIO

ACETIC ACID   56
ALKALI (OR BASE)   33, 56, 79, 80, 81
ALUM   42, 46, 51 to 59, 60 to 64
ANIMAL FIBRE   29, 34, 51 to 64, 73, 74, 79
CELLULOSE FIBRES   74
CITRIC ACID   (see acidic acid)
CHEMICAL REDUCTION   (see pH)
CHROMA   51, 65, 68
COMPLIMENTARY COLOURS   68, 69
CREAM OF TARTAR   42, 46, 51, 52
DEPTH OF SHADE   71
DYE STOCK SOLUTION   67, 77, 79
FASTNESS   43, 47, 73
HAZARDOUS MORDANT   31, 32, 41 to 47, 50 to52, 73
HUE   49, 74
LEVELING AGENT   51
LIGHTFASTNESS   (see fastness)
LYE   48, 61, 74, 80, 81
MORDANT   31, 32, 41 to 47, 50 to 53, 73
NATURAL DYES   39, 41, 42, 47
NATURAL FERMENTATION   80, 81
SAFE MORDANTS   (see mordant)
SCOURING   28, 30 to 34, 45, 73, 81
SECONDARY COLOURS   67, 68, 71, 79
pH   40, 41, 79, 80
PRIMARY COLOURS   67, 68, 79
TERTIARY COLOURS   68, 70, 79
VALUE   67, 68
VAT DYES   80

A FIBRE ARTIST OF THE LOOM

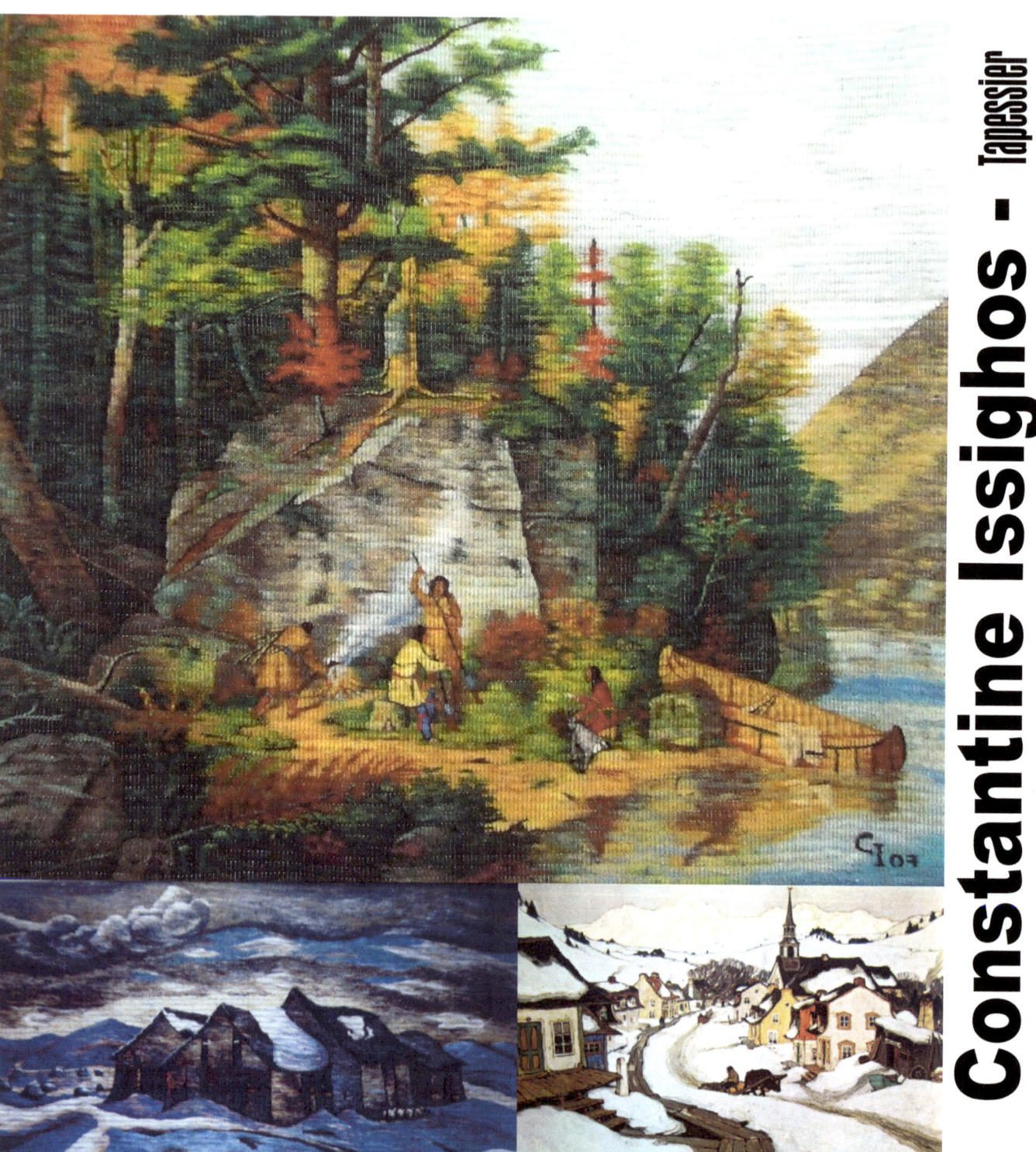

Constantine Issighos - Tapessier

FOR THE INSPIRED ARTIST OF THE LOOM
Beginner to Advance Level Illustrated Instructions

Constantine Issighos - Tapessier

GIVE A LIFE TIME GIFT TO YOUR FRIENDS AND COLLEAGUES

How I Built MY SIX-SIDED LOG HOME from scratch
MORTGAGE FREE!!!

Like yourself, the author to had a dream to build his own lot home from scratch. This book, with its real-life pictures, diagrams and actual copies of blueprints is the proof because the author has done it himself. Be prepared to think outside the box, when it comes to an unconventional method of financing your construction. When you, the reader, finish reading this book, you will no longer need to go before a lender with cap in hand to ask for a mortgage.

With over 300 full colour pictures, illustrations, and real-life events. This is an inspirational book of self-reliance and personal achievement.

(272 pages)

FULL COLOUR ILLUSTRATIONS!!

IN HARD COVER

NOW IN PAPERBACK!!

This book is one of its kind, because it is written about an equally one of a kind log home; a six-sided log home. This is a smart book – informal, unconventional in its approach. It helps the reader to understand that you do not need a mortgage hanging over your head in order to build this or any other style of log home. The author will guide you through beginning stage of getting started, how to purchase the right kind if building lot, planning and designing your project, to the final phase of construction.

A 272 page (in black tone) with over 300 real-life pictures and actual copies of this house, this inspirational book will take the reader through an easy to follow step-by-step guide.

BUILD IT MORTGAGE FREE!!

BUILD IT MORTGAGE FREE!!

BUILD YOUR LOG HOME MORTGAGE FREE!!

This is a working copy for every day use. This book is a condensed version, which contains all the essential construction information – with easy to follow step-by-step instructions and illustrations. This book contains:

- A copy of the actual blueprints of the six-sided log home.
- Design for a two – story round log home and of a small cabin.
- A glossary of construction, plumbing, and logging tools and terms.
- An inspirational narrative of actual events and wisdom.

A paperback edition.

YOUR SITE COPY

CD-ROM
How I Built MY SIX-SIDED LOG HOME from scratch

Contains the entire text of "My Six-Sided Log Home" with all its easy to follow step by step guide and over 300 colour illustrations.

(PDF Format)

PC/MAC

To purchase these books: www.awaqkunabooks.com

www.ingramcontent.com/pod-product-compliance
Lightning Source LLC
Chambersburg PA
CBHW040909020526
44116CB00026B/13